D0872406

Having a Career Day

Having a Career Day

101 Incredible Baseball Feats

STAN FISCHLER

SPORTS PUBLISHING

Sports Publishing books may be purchased in bulk at special discounts for sales promotion, corporate gifts, fund-raising, or educational purposes. Special editions can also be created to specifications. For details, contact the Special Sales Department, Sports Publishing, 307 West 36th Street, 11th Floor, New York, NY 10018 or sportspubbooks@skyhorsepublishing.com.

Sports Publishing® is a registered trademark of Skyhorse Publishing, Inc.®, a Delaware corporation.

All drawings by Joe Sinnott.

Baseball logos courtesy of Thinkstock.

Visit our website at www.sportspubbooks.com.

10 9 8 7 6 5 4 3 2 1

Library of Congress Cataloging-in-Publication Data is available on file.

Cover design by Brian Peterson
Cover photo credit AP Images

ISBN: 978-1-61321-684-2
Ebook ISBN: 978-1-61321-688-0

Printed in the United States of America

Dedication

Over the years I've had the privilege to work with some of the finest baseball people in the pro ranks, but the ones whom I have enjoyed most are special fans, and four in particular.

With that in mind, I hereby dedicate this work to the following:

* **Joe Sinnott** not only is the brilliant artist responsible for so many Spiderman works, but he also has done many excellent baseball drawings (see inside) and knows the game inside and out. Joe starred for the Saugerties, NY, high school varsity team and assorted other Catskill outfits after he returned from his South Pacific stint with the Navy Seabees. Joe and I have spent many memorable afternoons chatting baseball at Deising's superb eatery in Kingston.

My only gripe with Sinnott is the fact that he never cured himself of being a New York Giants fan.

* **Laurie Hemberger** is a scholar, a professor at Columbia University, and one of the best friends a neighbor ever had. Unlike Sinnott, Laurie has had the wisdom to be a lifelong rooter for the

St. Louis Cardinals. No less impressive is the fact that Hemberger's parents were friends of Stan (The Man) Musial, my all-time favorite Cardinal. During the Cards' run to their last World Series, Laurie and I had the pleasure of rooting through the downs and ups right up to our hailing their mighty victory.

* **The Sultan of Sonic Soul** happens to be my Catskill Mountain neighbor in Boiceville. Otherwise known as Gus Mancini, the man makes the most beautiful music out of his assorted saxophones and regularly entertains our Catskill neighbors on WDST Radio as well as gigs at local nightclubs and restaurants. Most of all, Gus–like Brother Joe Sinnott–was a Brooklyn high school baseball ace at Lafayette High in Bensonhurst. The Sultan's ever-lovin' affection for the Brooklyn Dodgers never ceases to impress me. The Sultan's taste is impeccable; wish he could have helped Sinnott!

* **Nancy Schuckman**: During her years at Brooklyn College, Nancy was as good a female shortstop as anyone had ever seen in Kings County. When I began watching her play in the Catskill town of Olive Women's Softball League, the elementary school principal from East New York had moved over to the hot corner. As a third base-woman, Nancy pulled off some of the most sensational fielding plays I'd ever seen by anyone, male or female. Better still, she proved to be an admirable neighbor and dear friend, especially at Tiso's Trattorio in Mount Tremper and Hoffman House in Kingston, not to mention our dining room.

My list could go on forever, but the aforementioned four are folks who have shared my love of the diamond pastime in unique, special ways. Love to them all.

Contents

II FASCINATING CHARACTERS

III UNLIKELY HEROES

IV INCREDIBLE FEATS

V OUTRAGEOUS

Introduction (Or Why I Wrote This Book)

I love baseball the way I love a double vanilla ice cream cone. This affection began very early in my life. Ebbets Field, home of the Brooklyn Dodgers, was the site of the first Major League game that I ever witnessed live.

It was June 1937. I was all of five years old and taken by my mother to the famed ballpark at Bedford Avenue and Sullivan Place (now occupied by a middle-income housing development).

Brooklyn was playing Pittsburgh that afternoon: an ordinary game, which seemed extraordinary to me. For one thing, I was fascinated by the ballpark's architecture. We entered through a majestic rotunda and then made our way to the left field grandstands by way of sloping concrete ramps.

From our seats we looked out on to a cozy diamond and straight ahead to the impressive right field scoreboard. I don't remember who won the game, but I do recall that Leo Durocher was at shortstop for Brooklyn—don't ask why I remember that—and the hot dogs were broiled, something I found appalling at the time and still do.

From that point on, baseball became as much a part of my life as Public School 54, Tom Mix on the radio, and building model airplanes.

By 1939, I had become a baseball picture card fanatic. Off-hours were spent at Al and Shirley's candy store on the corner of Nostrand and Vernon Avenues. When the boys weren't sipping Frank's (12 ounce) Orange Soda, we were plopping down our pennies to purchase baseball bubble gum picture cards.

We paid no mind to the Fleer's bubble-gum—tossed it away, actually—but plucked the coveted cards. My favorites hardly were legends. I liked Ernest Gordon (Babe) Phelps, the Dodgers catcher, and Stanley (Frenchy) Bordegaray best.

After buying the cards, our standard sidewalk game consisted of card-flipping. First, one of the lads would flip his card on the sidewalk. Then, his opponent would do likewise. If they matched, the second flipper "won" the other's card. Otherwise, the vice was versa.

I diligently followed the Major League races via my father's favorite newspaper, (the *World-Telegram*), which was the Scripps-Howard flagship evening broad sheet. Its baseball writers included Dan Daniel and Bill Roeder, while Willard Mullin penned the best sports cartoons ever drawn. What I didn't learn about baseball from the papers, I got on the radio via the voice of the Dodgers, Rod Barber, who was still considered the best in the business.

By 1940, the Dodgers had been built into a National League pennant contender and Brooklyn had become—or so we thought—the baseball mecca of the whole, wide world. First baseman Dolph Camilli was poling home runs over the right field fence and onto Bedford Avenue, Whitlow Wyatt starred on the mound, and a Southerner named Fred (Dixie) Walker had emerged as what Brooklynites called "The People's Cherce."

We didn't win the pennant in 1940, but a year later manager Leo (The Lip) Durocher piloted the Brooks—also called "The Flock"—to the borough's first pennant since 1920.

Alas, tragedy struck in the World Series. Trailing two games to one to the hated Yankees, the Brooks appeared to have the game wrapped up, leading with two out in the Bombers' ninth. Subsequently, reliever Hugh Casey threw a harsh curve—some say a spitball—to Tommy Henrich for the third strike and, seemingly, a Dodgers win.

But the ball eluded catcher Mickey Owen, Henrich raced safely to first, and from there the Dodgers completely collapsed. The Yankees rallied for the win and took the Series in five games. For Brooklynites such as myself, it was a borough-wide tragedy that never will be forgotten.

The Casey-Owen blunder left a scar on my baseball-rooting conscience all winter, and by spring training, I had made what was then a monumental decision. I decided to switch my rooting allegiance to the St. Louis Cardinals.

This was easy. They had a Stan in the lineup—Stan (The Man) Musial—and he wore my favorite number, six. I also loved the logo, featuring a cardinal sitting on a baseball bat.

The year 1942 was the best time to become a Cardinals fan. With a lineup sprinkling with such hustlers as Enos (Country) Slaughter, Marty (Slats) Marion, and George (Whitey) Kurowski, the Cards became known as "The St. Louis Swifties."

And what a pitching staff they had. Morton Cooper, Howie Pollet, Johnny Beazley, and Max Lanier combined to give manager Billy Southworth the best mound unit in baseball.

These elements blended to produce what Mister Baseball, Connie Mack, called "the greatest team in baseball history."

Naturally, I ate this all up as the Cards rampaged through the homestretch to beat Brooklyn and win the pennant.

During that run to the flag, I enjoyed one game more than any. It took place during the summer of 1942, at Ebbets Field with my best friend, Howie Sparer, who was then a Dodgers fan.

A Cardinals-Dodgers game was always special in those days, but this one had an extra added quality to it because the best pitcher on each team—Whitlow Wyatt of Brooklyn and Morton Cooper of St. Louis—was facing the other.

That, however, was secondary to our capturing our seats and then my opening my Lone Ranger lunchbox and, most importantly, its Thermos bottle. I gingerly flipped the clamp on the outside, lifted the lunchbox cover, and then grasped the Thermos.

Finally, I heaved a sigh of relief as the cork came off. Inside, I could see the amber, sparkling cola which I eagerly poured into the cup. It was the best Pepsi-Cola I had ever tasted!

The same could be said of the ball game. The Cards and Dodgers were tied 0–0 going into the top of the ninth, when St. Louis third baseman Whitey Kurowski, one of my favorites, belted a Wyatt fastball into the lower left field grandstand. Cooper shut out the Brooks in the bottom of the ninth and it ended 1–0 for the Cardinals. My team had won, Howie's had lost, and the whole package—soda, weather, result—made it one of the best baseball days of my life.

When the Dodgers were on the road, my dad would take me to a different kind of ballpark with different kinds of players.

The baseball stadium in question was called Dexter Park, which sat on the border of Brooklyn and Queens. For decades, Dexter Park was regarded as one of the finest minor league fields in the country.

Its home team—the Bushwicks—was regarded as "semipro," but in reality the club was on a par with the Triple-A International League teams. Managed by Joe Press, the Bushwicks played the best of the African American teams of the 1930s and 1940s.

This was prior to Jackie Robinson breaking the color barrier in Brooklyn and that meant some of the finest players in baseball appeared on the rosters of the Negro National League and Negro American League teams that played the Bushwicks at Dexter Park.

On any given Sunday, I had the pleasure of watching such legendary African American stars as Satchel Paige, Roy Campanella, and Josh Gibson going up against the Bushwicks, who always featured a couple of former Major Leaguers on their roster.

The ambience at Dexter Park had the relaxed, homey feeling of a Minor League game, but the competition was keen and for half a buck, who could complain?

Once the Dodgers returned from their road trips, we would bid au revoir to Dexter Field action and again focus on the Major League races.

My affection for the Cardinals was momentarily diluted during the 1944 World Series. In addition to St. Louis' National League team, what's known as "The Mound City" also had an American League club, the Browns. And I loved them equally as well in 1944 when they won their one and only pennant and faced the Cards in the World Series. Since I always rooted for underdogs, I chose to back the Brownies, who, alas, had a two-games-to-one lead, but blew it and went down in six.

Once the war ended, I continued supporting the Cardinals and enjoyed one more unforgettable day—a doubleheader at the Polo Grounds in 1946, Cards vs. Giants. By this time, St.Louis had acquired a handsome first baseman named Vernal (Nippy) Jones.

On that Sunday afternoon in Harlem, Jones had the doubleheader of his life. He went something like five-for-five in the opener and five-for-six in the second game. The Cards won both, but that wasn't the whole story. After the game, fans were allowed to walk past the outfield and onto the street behind the clubhouse.

Someone tipped me off that if I hung around long enough, I would see the players come down the steps from their dressing room and that I could get autographs. That suited me fine because

I always remembered the first Cards autograph I got outside Ebbets Field a few years earlier. The signature belonged to one of my favorite pitchers, Harry (The Cat) Brecheen, and the other thing I recalled about The Cat was that he was wearing the pointiest shoes I had ever seen: beautiful brown Florsheims.

I soon realized that my tipster was right. One by one the Cardinals stepped out of the clubhouse door and down the metal steps to the sidewalk. By rights I should have pursued the autograph of Stan (The Man) Musial, my favorite Cardinal, but instead, I sought Nippy Jones. And, sure enough, his black curly hair still sparkling in the sunlight from his shower, Jones walked down and graciously signed my book. That autograph made my one-hour subway ride home one of the most pleasant of my young life.

Much as I adored the Cardinals, my latent affection for our home team, the Dodgers, returned by 1950 and I found myself rooting for Brooklyn once again. These were the golden years of what author Roger Kahn later called "The Boys of Summer" from his book of the same name.

It was a glorious collection of athletes, one which inspired my pal and Dodgers press agent Irving Rudd to note, "There's not a rotter in the lot."

Trouble is, they had troubles. The Giants outed them in a memorable Bobby Thomson "Shot Heard Round The World" 1951 playoff, and when Brooklyn finally did win the pennant, the Yankees annually knocked them out in the World Series.

Revenge finally came in 1955, my first year as a full-time sportswriter for Hearst's evening daily, the *New York Journal-American*. That was *the* year for the Brooks.

After losing the first pair of games in the Bronx, the Dodgers returned home for Game Three, one of the most exciting I ever attended. Led by Duke Snider's big bat, Dem Bums routed the

Bombers, and we had a series. It went to seven games, and in the finale Johnny Podres from Upstate New York pitched a beauty and Sandy Amoros made one of the best catches in Series annals and, for a change, we Brooklyn fans did not have to "wait 'til next year."

My last memorable thrill as a newsman emerged in 1969, when I covered the New York Mets for the late lamented *Suffolk Sun*, a Cowles daily with great promise that never was fully realized.

Not that I'm a baseball *maven*, but down the homestretch I sensed something special about the Mets' karma. If there was a break to be had, it would break in the Mets' favor and it eventually carried into the World Series triumph—first for the franchise—at Shea Stadium.

I had the good fortune to be just a few feet away from winning manager—ex-Brooklyn first base hero—Gil Hodges when President Richard Nixon phoned him from the White House for congratulations. For me—newsman and baseball fan—that was as good as it could get.

In my later years—starting in 1998, to be exact—I unswervingly switched my allegiance to the Oakland Athletics. What arrested my attention was the adroit manner in which general manager Billy Beane managed to produce competitive teams despite an extraordinarily law budget.

I also found favorite players, such as pitcher Gil Heredia, whom I had the pleasure of interviewing in the A's' dugout pregame at Yankee Stadium. My latest Oakland hero is Coco Crisp in the outfield. All of which must tell you by now the most obvious thing of all. That is, my love of baseball, which began as a kid growing up in Brooklyn, has remained with me to this day.

Adoring our national pastime with a passion made it pretty darn easy for me to write this book. I hope you enjoy it as much as I had fun writing it.

Acknowledgments

Many good folks were behind the scenes helping me put this book together. The saga started with my delightful editor, Julie Ganz, encouraging me to take on the project.

For the research and development, aides in my office helped with an assortment of literary "relief pitching." These include the likes of Scott Charles, Allyson Gronowitz, Adrian Szkolar, Jaclyn Matisak, Michael Cotton, Kirsten Ambrosio, Darren Im, Rakhee Kulkarni, Steve Simineri, Ricky Cibrano, Al Zelazo, and Mike Valente.

Having a Career Day

I
Baseball History

1 | THE MOST INCREDIBLE RELIEF JOB IN HISTORY

Later to become a respected umpire, Ed Rommel was a thirty-five-year-old relief pitcher for the Philadelphia Athletics, sitting in the bullpen on the afternoon of June 10, 1932. The Athletics were facing the Cleveland Indians, and before the veteran Rommel could get comfortable, he was summoned in the second inning after the starter failed.

At the time, Philadelphia was trailing Cleveland, 3–2, and Rommel could not have dreamed what would unfold in the next *four hours and seventeen innings.* At that end of that period, Rommel staggered toward the dugout as the winning hurler. Granted, he had given up twenty-nine hits and fourteen runs, but he won the contest, 18–17.

No other reliever could make that statement.

In retrospect, perhaps that explains why Ed Rommel became an umpire.

2 | FELLER'S BID FOR A WIN FELLED IN A STRANGE WAY

Bob Feller is one Hall of Famer who had a right to sing the blues after one of the most incredible performances in diamond annals. Facing Detroit on October 2, 1938, the man who became known as Rapid Robert did allow seven hits, but he also struck out *eighteen* Detroit batsmen, setting what was then an all-time Major League record. Yet, despite that incredible feat, he lost the game, 4–1, to the Tigers, proving on that day that justice does not always triumph on the mound.

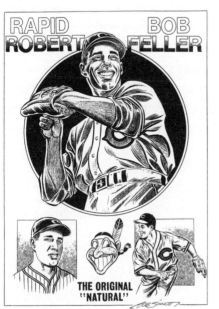

RAPID ROBERT BOB FELLER

THE ORIGINAL "NATURAL"

3 | FOUR HOME RUNS THE ODD WAY

Ed Delahanty of the Phillies was the first Major Leaguer to hit four home runs in a single game. But the slugger did it the odd way.

Two of Ed's first three round-trippers were inside-the-park clouds. The reason: the ball rolled into the area way under the clubhouse.

Prior to the fourth four-bagger, Bill Lange of the Chicago Colts dashed back under the clubhouse as a joke.

This time, Delahanty smote a line drive to right-center field. Before wise guy Lange could climb out from under the clubhouse, Delahanty had circled the bases to make it a quartet of round-trippers in a roundabout sort of way!

4 | WILLIE MAYS' INCREDIBLE CATCH HIJACKS A SERIES

I f a single catch can "steal" a World Series for a baseball club, New York Giants center fielder Willie Mays pulled off such a feat at the Polo Grounds in Manhattan's Harlem.

Mays, also known as "The Say Hey Kid," was one of the most arresting players ever to step on a diamond. The Giants superstar could make game-changing plays at the plate, on the base paths, or in the field. Mays manned center field in stellar fashion.

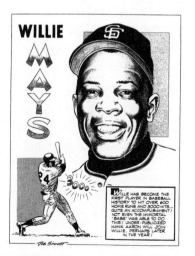

WILLIE
MAYS

WILLIE HAS BECOME THE
FIRST PLAYER IN BASEBALL
HISTORY TO HIT OVER 600
HOME RUNS AND 3000 HITS...
QUITE AN ACCOMPLISHMENT!
NOT EVEN THE IMMORTAL
'BABE' WAS ABLE TO DO
THIS! UNDER-PUBLICIZED
HANK AARON WILL JOIN
WILLIE, PERHAPS LATER
IN THE YEAR!

But the most electrifying play came in Game One of the 1954 World Series—a play that has defined Mays' career.

The New York Giants had put together a pretty darn good season, but their opponents, the Cleveland Indians, had managed to put together an even better one.

The Indians shattered the league record for wins at the time, earning 111 victories. The club was the clear favorite heading into the Series. After all, how could one of the best teams of all time come all this way to lose?

Game One at the Polo Grounds was a tightly contested matchup. By the time the eighth inning rolled around, the score was tied 2–2. However, the Indians were threatening. The first two hitters reached base safely, on a walk and single respectively. With Larry Doby standing at second as the potential go-ahead run, Vic Wertz approached the dish.

Wertz had already done damage in the game, driving in both of the Indians' runs back in the first inning. Facing Don Liddle in the eighth, Wertz had a chance to drive in two more.

Wertz jumped all over Liddle's first pitch and drove it to deep center. The ball soared in the air, too deep for Mays to just simply backtrack on it. So, he took a risk and did a 360 degree turn, with his back completely facing the infield. Mays was nearly 450 feet from home when he reached his glove out in front of his left shoulder. Amazingly, he caught the ball. Even more amazing was that he immediately turned around and fired a strike to second base to double up Doby.

Mays gave the Giants a second life, and the team took advantage of it. The Giants went on to win that game in the tenth inning—and then win the next three contests to capture a World Series title. They had stunned the Indians and baseball.

Although "The Catch" happened in the first game, some claim Mays' acrobatic play gave the Giants enough momentum to stop the Indians in their tracks and capture the Series. Incredible, but true!

5 | A PERFECT CASE OF PITCHING LARCENY BY DON LARSEN

Don Larsen certainly wasn't the worst pitcher, but nor was he the best. That's why the outcome of Game Five of the 1956 World Series took the baseball world completely by surprise.

The beginning of Larsen's career was highlighted by his antics off the field, rather than his performance on it. It was known that Larsen liked to have a good time in his extracurricular life, but his 10–33 record through his first two seasons didn't suggest that he was to have a good time on the mound.

The St. Louis Browns then traded Larsen to the New York Yankees prior to the 1955 season, and things were beginning to look up.

Larsen won eleven games for the Yankees, although he had yet to prove that he could be consistent. Larsen pitched well in the last four starts of the season, so when the Yankees captured the American League pennant, Larsen had a spot in the rotation in the World Series against the Brooklyn Dodgers.

Despite the promise Larsen showed in previous starts, he regressed in Game Two. He failed to make it past the second inning, leading to a 13–8 Dodgers' victory. Fast-forward to Game Five. The Yankees had managed to even the series at two games apiece. The team that won Game Five would be only a game away from a World Championship. Given the situation, Larsen had a lot on his plate. This time, the Yankees needed Larsen to go more than just two innings.

The stage was set. Yankee Stadium was packed. Mickey Mantle gave fans a treat when he homered in the fourth for the Yankees' first hit and run of the game. Up to this point, Larsen had yet to allow a runner on base. Another run for the Yanks in the sixth gave Larsen a two-run cushion. The Yankees appeared to be on their way to a win. As the game came closer to a finish, though, a potential win wasn't what fans were buzzing about. More than sixty-four thousand people grew increasingly aware that they may see something that had never been done before.

By the ninth inning, no Dodger had recorded a hit. No Yankee fielder had made an error. No Dodger had reached base. A perfect game was on the line, and three hitters were standing in Larsen's way. First batter up: Carl Furillo. Fly out. *One out*. Roy Campanella settled in next. Ground out. *Two outs.* Dale Mitchell came to the plate as a pinch hitter. He was a dangerous hitter who rarely struck out. That didn't phase Larsen. He got two strikes on him. The final pitch of the game was a fastball on the lower outside part of the plate. Mitchell checked his swing, but that didn't matter. Home plate umpire, Babe Pinelli, called it strike three anyway. *Three outs*. Game over! Euphoria for Larsen and his teammates.

Larsen, who had been haunted by mediocrity, had done the unimaginable. He threw the first—and to this day only—perfect game in World Series history. His achievement is considered by many to be the most memorable performance in World Series history. Catcher Yogi Berra leaping into Larsen's arms in celebration made for one of the most iconic images in sports to this day.

The Yankees went on to win the series in seven games, but the 1956 World Series isn't often remembered for the victor, but rather for the man who gave his team a boost when they needed it most.

6 | ONE MANAGER COMES, ONE MANAGER GOES IN A DEAL

Trades in baseball happen as often as relief pitchers yawn in the bullpen. But it's a case of man-biting-dog when one manager gets traded for another dugout boss. How did it happen?

On August 3, 1960, an unprecedented swap of managers took place when Joe Gordon of the Cleveland Indians and Jimmy Dykes of the Detroit Tigers switched jobs. At the time, the Indians were in fourth place and the Tigers sixth. Bill DeWitt, then Tigers' president, said he proposed the trade as a joke in a conversation with Frank Lane, Cleveland's general manager. "We were discussing player trades," DeWitt recalled. "I said, 'Frank, we're getting nowhere on this, so let's trade managers.' I meant it to be facetious." Lane, one of the greatest wheeler-dealers, later said, "I considered Bill's remark in a jocular vein. But then the way we began to stumble, it became no joke to me." On the day the managerial switch was arranged, the Indians had lost for the fourteenth time in their last eighteen games.

The swap didn't help either club. Detroit never climbed out of sixth place and Gordon was fired at the end of the year. After finishing fourth with the Indians in 1960, Dykes lasted through the 1961 season when he, too, was fired.

7 | A DOUBLE PLAY COMBINATION IS IMMORTALIZED IN POETRY

One of the all-time best infield combinations belonged to the Chicago Cubs. It was in fact so good that it inspired author Franklin Pierce Adams to dash off some poetry.

The combination was Tinker, Evers, and Chance. Usually, the double play began with a ground ball to shortstop Tinker, who relayed the ball to second baseman Evers, who then pegged the ball to first baseman Chance. In his poem, "Baseball's Sad Lexicon," Adams penned the following:

Ruthlessly pricking our gonfalon bubble,

Making a Giant hit into a double,

Words that are weighty with nothing but trouble:

"Tinker to Evers to Chance."

8 | INCREDIBLY, A PITCHER PRODUCED A 2.60 EARNED RUN AVERAGE BUT FINISHED THE SEASON WITH NOTHING BETTER THAN A .500 RECORD

Pitching for the Detroit Tigers, George Mullin had to wonder what he needed to do when it came to winning games.

On the one hand, he was one of the best hurlers in Major League Baseball and had the earned run average to prove it. But that didn't seem to matter.

In 1907, he finished with a 20–20 record, starting forty-two games and completing thirty-five. Mullin did improve his statistics. In 1908 he won twenty-four and lost twelve, with a 1.94 ERA. In 1909, he won twenty-nine and lost nine, with a 2.22 ERA, to lead the league in winning percentage and in wins.

"Wabash George," who was born on July 4, 1880, also played second base and the outfield. In 1913 he suffered a terrible year. He jumped to the Federal League in 1914 and concluded his career with the "Feds." He had a lifetime record of 228–196, including his time with the "Feds."

For a pitcher to win twenty or more games and also lose twenty or more in the same season is not that rare. The Atlanta Braves' Phil Niekro, for example, won twenty-one and lost twenty in 1979.

Speaking of remarkable records, how about Joel Horlen's 2.43 ERA with the Chicago White Sox in 1966, when his record was 10–13? That same year Gary Peters of the White Sox produced a 1.98 ERA and a 12–10 record. In 1978, Steve Rogers of the Montreal Expos had a 2.45 ERA and an 11–13 record. He was beaten by Craig Swan of the New York Mets, who had a 2.43 ERA and a 9–6 record.

9 | OVERCOMING AN EIGHT-RUN DEFICIT IN THE SEVENTH INNING OF A WORLD SERIES GAME TO WIN THE CONTEST

Naturally, the Chicago Cubs proved to be the victims against the Philadelphia Athletics.

It was the fourth game of the 1929 World Series at Philadelphia.

Charlie Root was on the mound for the Cubs in the bottom half of the seventh inning.

The A's were behind 8–0 with Al Simmons at the plate. Simmons, who boasted a .365 batting average that year, with thirty-four home runs and a towering 157 runs batted in, was in vintage form.

He smashed a home run onto the roof of the Stadium's left field stands. The Score was now 8–1 Chicago.

This brought up Jimmy Foxx, a man who hit thirty-three homers that year, along with a sizzling .354 batting average and 117 runs batted in. Foxx singled to right field. That was followed by a single from Bing Miller, which was lost in the sun by veteran Hack Wilson as Foxx sped to third.

Jimmy Dykes also singled, scoring Foxx and moving Miller to second. The score was now 8–2 Chicago. Next, Joe Boley singled for the fifth consecutive Philadelphia hit, scoring Miller. The score now was 8–3, Chicago.

Connie Mack, the A's manager, knew a good thing when he saw it. He yanked his next hitter, pitcher Ed Rommel, and sent George Burns in to pinch-hit. Burns popped up for the first out. One down. But Max Bishop followed with a bloop single. Another run scored, and now it was 8–4, Chicago, with two on and one out.

That was enough for Cubs manager Joe McCarthy. He yanked Charlie Root and replaced him with Art Nehf, who had a 5.58 earned run average and an 8–5 record. Nehf took his warm-up tosses and then faced Mule Haas, who proceeded to belt a hard line drive that Hack Wilson lost in the sun as it went by him to the wall. By the time Wilson retrieved the ball and fired it home, Haas had a three-run, inside-the-park home run. The score was now 8–7, and the fans were on their feet, screaming.

Mickey Cochrane, the great Athletics catcher, was walked. McCarthy gave Nehf the hook and replaced him with Sheriff Blake, who was 14–13 with a 4.20 earned run average. Blake allowed Al Simmons (the A's now had batted around) a single over third sacker Norm MacMillan's head, and Cochrane reached second. Jimmy Foxx then singled again, and the ball game was tied 8–8.

Enraged, McCarthy brought in his ace, Pat Malone, who had a 22–10 record with a 3.57 ERA. Malone was wild and immediately hit Bing Miller to load the bases. McCarthy stayed with Malone, whereupon Jimmy Dykes slammed a double to the left field wall. Simmons and Foxx scored to make it 10–8, A's. At last, Malone disposed of Boley and Burns, the pinch hitter coming up for his second at bat. The final score was 10–8, A's. Philadelphia won the Series in five games.

10 | WHO WON THE 1945 ALL-STAR GAME?

For the first time since its inception in 1933, there was no All-Star Game winner in 1945.

Why did Baseball Commissioner Happy Chandler cancel the midsummer tradition?

Because so many genuine All-Stars had departed to fight in World War II, the game was replaced with exhibition contests played between Major League teams and Minor League teams, military clubs, and college teams.

The proceeds were diverted to the war effort. The All-Star Game was reinstated in 1946, when the American League defeated the National League, 12–0, at Fenway Park in Boston.

11 | WHY DID THREE CRUCIAL PLAYERS IN THE 1947 WORLD SERIES NEVER PLAY ANOTHER BIG LEAGUE GAME?

n 1947, heated rivals—the New York Yankees and the Brooklyn Dodgers—faced off in the World Series.

But the Series would mark the final professional games for three key players. Can you recall any of their names?

In Game Four, Bill Bevens of the Bombers and Harry Taylor of the Brooks squared off at Ebbets Field. Taylor was quickly knocked out of the game and replaced by Hal Gregg. But Bevens rolled mightily along, allowing one run, ten walks, a wild pitch, and incredibly, not a single hit through eight innings.

In the bottom of the ninth, Carl Furillo of the Dodgers was walked with one out. Al Gionfriddo was sent in to run for Furillo. With two outs, pinch hitter Pistol Pete Reiser, who was suffering from a lame ankle, stepped into the batter's box. Reiser was intentionally walked to bring up weak-hitting Eddie Stanky. But he never made it to the plate.

Stanky was replaced by ancient third baseman Cookie Lavagetto, who responded with a line drive that bounced off the right field wall to score Gionfriddo, as well as Eddie Miksis, who had been sent in to run for Reiser.

Lavagetto's double won the game for Brooklyn, 3–2. Bevens had lost a no-hitter as well as a World Series one-hitter in the bottom of the ninth.

Although both appeared again over the course of the Series, neither Bevens nor Lavagetto would play in another regular-season game.

Bevens had had a poor year and decided to conclude his four-year career after the Series. Meanwhile, Lavagetto was winding down a fourteen-year career, ten of them with the Dodgers. He retired after the season with a tidy .300 lifetime average.

Gionfriddo, the third man in the group, also factored significantly in the outcome of the Series. His shining moment came in Game Six at Yankee Stadium. With two on and two out in the bottom of the sixth, Joe DiMaggio drove a deep fly ball that appeared to be headed for the bleachers, until Gionfriddo flagged it down at the 415-foot sign in front of the bullpen.

As the stoical DiMaggio rounded first, he saw the ball slam into Gionfriddo's glove. The Yankee Clipper then betrayed visible emotion for one of the few times in his career, kicking at the dirt before returning to the bench. The catch saved the sixth game and kept Dodger hurler Joe Hatten alive.

Gionfriddo was concluding a four-year Major League career, which included stints in Pittsburgh and Brooklyn. In thirty-seven games with the Brooks in 1947, he hit just .177. But his catch helped the Dodgers tie the Series and force Game Seven. He was never heard from again.

The Yankees ultimately prevailed in the seventh game as Gionfriddo, Bevens, and Lavagetto saw their names inscribed in the books before departing from the game forever.

12 | THE BROTHER ACT THAT WON FORTY-FIVE GAMES IN ONE SEASON

In the early 1930s, the St. Louis Cardinals were known as baseball's Gashouse Gang.

Among their leaders were the pitching brothers act of Dizzy Dean and his brother, Paul.

They learned the game in their native Arkansas.

When they arrived at spring training in 1934, Dizzy grabbed a bunch of baseball writers and declared, "Me 'n' Paul is gonna win forty-five games this year."

While he was at it, Dizzy also predicted that the Cardinals would win the National League pennant.

So, what happened? Dizzy and Paul made good on the promise. The brothers racked up forty-nine victories that year: thirty by Dizzy and nineteen by Paul. Next, in the World Series against the favored Detroit Tigers, Diz declared: "Me 'n' Paul can beat 'em all by us-selves." And they did, with each brother winning two games!

Another time, when Dizzy pitched a three-hit shutout in the first game of a doubleheader against the Dodgers, Paul came back *with a no-hitter in the nightcap.* "Shucks," said Diz after the game. "If I'd knowed Paul was gonna pitch a no-hitter, why I'd a pitched a no-hitter too."

13 | NOLAN RYAN'S RECORD SEVEN NO-HITTERS

There are only a handful of records in sports that you can truly say are untouchable, and Ryan's record seven no-hitters is one of them. Throwing one is incredible, two is phenomenal, and three is rarified air, but seven? That's just crazy talk.

Only twenty-two pitchers have thrown multiple no-hitters, and of those twenty-two, only two other than Ryan have tossed more than two–Sandy Koufax and Bob Feller. Koufax is second with four, three fewer than the Ryan Express. Perhaps it's best to think of it this way when explaining just how far ahead of the pack Ryan is. Ryan's seven no-no's is a 43 percent increase over the second-place Koufax's four.

If a player were to break Hank Aaron's legitimate all-time home run record of 755 by 43 percent, he would need to hit (roughly) 1,324 home runs, 569 more than Aaron. When it comes to no-hitters, Ryan didn't just lap the field; he blew everyone else out of the water.

In the history of Major League Baseball, there have been just 281 no-no's. That's in well over one hundred thousand total games—just 281. The fact is, it is a very rare occurrence, and throwing even one is an incredibly hard thing to do. Just look at the list of pitchers who went their *entire careers* without throwing even one no-hitter: Grover Cleveland Alexander, Greg Maddux, Pedro Martinez, Lefty Grove, and Steve Carlton, among others.

The aforementioned men have a combined seven World Series rings, eleven Cy Youngs (keep in mind the award didn't exist in Alexander and Grove's day), and an MVP—yet not a single no-hitter.

For a no-hitter to take place, three things are needed: a tremendous amount of skill, a massive amount of luck, and, if you are to throw seven like Ryan, incredible, almost unparalleled, longevity.

It's for these reasons that so few pitchers have thrown more than one, and so many great ones haven't thrown any at all. Nolan Ryan was quite literally made to throw no-hitters—he was a fireballer who minimized contact, yet had one of those once-in-a-lifetime arms that, despite all the innings and the sustained velocity, kept him from ever being seriously injured or losing much off his heater.

These factors allowed Ryan to catch lightning in a bottle not once, not twice, but an astonishing seven times—an incredible feat that may never be equaled.

14 | THE WORLD SERIES THAT HAD FANS EVENLY DIVIDED

In this era of fanatical home team devotion, it's hard to imagine a World Series that had fans split right down the middle. But it did happen in 1944 when the St. Louis Browns—normally inept—won the American League pennant for the one and only time in franchise history.

It turned out to be the first and only all-St. Louis World Series ever played; the Cardinals under Billy Southworth had won their third straight pennant. The Series was played at the home field for both clubs, Sportsmans Park. That fact had fans trying to figure out which team to root for, from game to game.

The Cardinals had always been the favorite because they had a consistent winning record.

On the other hand, the Brownies, managed by Luke Sewell, suddenly emerged as the Cinderella team, and fans just loved that. "It was the damnedest Series," the Browns manager said. "St. Louis fans seemed to be rooting for both teams. I've never seen games where, whatever either side did, [they] got the same amount of cheering."

15 | BASEBALL BILLBOARDS AS FAMOUS AS THE BALLPARKS

I n the history of Major League Baseball, one ballpark billboard emerged over the decades as the most famous and challenging of all.

Likewise, in the annals of Minor League ball, a billboard has long been regarded as the funniest of them all.

First we deal with Exhibit A: Ebbets Field, home of the Brooklyn Dodgers. Sitting at the bottom of the right field scoreboard was a sign about five feet high and forty feet wide.

It featured the name "Abe Stark," one of the most popular—if not *the* most—clothiers in Kings County.

Stark was so beloved that he eventually would go on and become borough president of Brooklyn for three terms and later became City Council president from 1954–1961.

But selling suits was his primary gig, and each side of the billboard had his favorite suit company, GGG.

Less notable were the words that became notorious throughout the diamond world. Situated just to the left of the "A" in "Abe" was a large arrow and the inscription "HIT SIGN, WIN SUIT."

To the naked eye, it looked exceedingly doable, but the fact of the matter is, not a single ballplayer was ever gifted a GGG suit, and there were good reasons for that.

On the one hand, few line drives would reach such a low level, and for another, Dodgers right fielder Carl Furillo was so adept at his profession that he would intercept any such blasts from opposing batters.

Abe Stark's sign even became the subject of a *New Yorker* cartoon.

For the sake of a laugh, the cartoonist moved Abe's sign to left field directly under the grandstand. Stark was depicted sitting in the front row wearing an outfielder's glove. As the ball was about to hit the sign, Abe was seen reaching over just in the nick of time, saving himself one freebie suit.

The Minor League gem was at Dexter Park on the Brooklyn-Queens border. It was home of the Brooklyn Buschwicks, one of the most famous independent teams in America.

Just to the left of the right field foul line was a billboard that read:

"DON'T KILL THE UMPIRE—MAYBE IT'S YOUR EYES—SEE GOLDBERG THE OPTICIAN."

16 | THE FASTEST BUILDING OF A BASEBALL CATHEDRAL

Everybody knows that Yankee Stadium has everlastingly been called "The House That Ruth Built."

That's Ruth, as in "the Babe."

But few realize who built the House That Ruth Built. And that happened to be the distinguished firm White Construction Company. Not only did the outfit do a phenomenal job in building the cathedral of the sport, but it was done in near record time.

Noted historian Jim Reisler documented some of the facts in the book, *Babe Ruth Slept Here: The Baseball Landmarks of New York City*.

Back in 1922, when $2.5 million was a lot of money instead of a year's salary for a mediocre utility infielder, a cathedral rose in the South Bronx. It was Yankee Stadium.

Work began without ceremony on May 6, 1922, on the 11.6-acre plot of land, purchased the year before from the William Waldorf Astor estate. It was directly across the river from the Polo Grounds, which the Yankees then shared with the Giants.

Workers had been on an ambitious work schedule, trying to complete the massive ballpark for the 1922 World Series. "A little teamwork will be necessary to accomplish this happy result," said Bernard Green, the engineer representing the Osborn Engineering

Company of Cleveland, which drew up the initial plans for the ballpark.

The teamwork was overmatched, and the new ballpark didn't make it for that fall's Yankees vs. Giants World Series. It was played entirely at the Polo Grounds.

But the ballpark was ready for the following season, turning some forty-five thousand cubic yards of earth, two thousand tons of steel, and eighteen thousand cubic yards of reinforced concrete into a three-tiered colossus of a ballpark. Yankee Stadium's grandstand and bleachers alone required six hundred thousand lineal feet of lumber, four miles of piping for rails, and five hundred tons of iron.

Opening ceremonies took place on April 23, 1923, under crystal blue skies before the Yankees took on Boston. The Babe, with characteristic timing, belted the ballpark's first home run—a three-run shot to right that iced a 4–1 Yankees' victory.

A capacity crowd of 74,200 crammed the new ballpark to the rafters for the opener. Another twenty-five thousand milled around outside, hoping to get in, but couldn't. The big crowd, which dwarfed baseball's previous record crowd of forty-two thousand, was orderly and got to and from the stadium, easily, thanks in part to the smooth working of the subway, "which handled the heavy traffic without a break," according to reports.

17 | HOW THE BEST BASEBALL CENTER IN THE WORLD BECAME A GHOST DIAMOND

Movies, songs, and standup comic routines prevailed over thirty years with Brooklyn and its baseball team, the Dodgers, as the prevailing theme.

Such flicks as *It Happened in Brooklyn* and vaudeville acts including the Abbott and Costello *Who's on First?* originated on Brooklyn stages.

The Dodgers were so popular that the ballplayers even formed a basketball team, playing on the stage of the huge Brooklyn Paramount Theater.

When the Dodgers won the National League pennant in 1941, they were far and away the most popular collection of baseball players the nation had known. And if anyone dared suggest that someday they would leave Brooklyn, a team of psychiatrists would instantly be summoned to treat the mad man.

For anyone old enough to remember watching the Brooklyn Dodgers play, the team's departure still stings more than half a century later. To some, the move to Los Angeles was like a stab in the back—a betrayal that evoked anger in the borough. But to many, heartbreak overshadowed anger.

For decades, the Dodgers brought excitement and joy to Brooklyn and the civilized world. The team unified the people of

Brooklyn and stirred the local economy. Ebbets Field, with all its quirks, was home to colorful Brooklyn inhabitants. The park was usually packed for home games, seating thirty-three thousand.

The fans let their presence be known too. When the fans were frustrated, the players knew. Brooklynites got on players' cases when they struggled, but at the end of the day, they always supported the athletes and were as loyal fans as you could find. Dodger baseball consumed Brooklyn. But that all changed in 1957.

When news of the end of Brooklyn baseball broke midway through the 1957 season, fans voiced their outrage. Despite their protests, team owner Walter O'Malley stood firm behind the move. The plan was set. The Dodgers would make the journey from one coast to another, leaving Brooklyn behind for Los Angeles.

The Dodgers played their last game in Brooklyn on September 24, 1957. The team's tenure in the borough ended on a high note, with the Dodgers shutting out the Pittsburgh Pirates 2–0—a day that all those in attendance would hold close to their hearts. The game wasn't the last event at the historic ballpark.

In February 1960, a ceremony was held to commemorate Ebbets Field before a wrecking ball demolished it. While some refused to attend because they couldn't bear to watch the demolition, about two hundred people showed up to say goodbye. Dodger greats Roy Campanella and Ralph Branca were among those to pay tribute.

Three years later, no remnants of a ballpark remained. Apartments opened in its place. Nevertheless, the memory of "Brooklyn's Cathedral" didn't disappear. The complex was aptly named "Ebbets Field Apartments."

18 | THE BASEBALL WAR TO END ALL WARS

The term "brotherhood" invariably has a positive meaning. But this was not always the case when it came to a battle in the earliest days of the diamond sport.

Not surprisingly to some, it was all about the organization of the earliest players union. The term associated with the upheaval was called "The Brotherhood War of 1885." It resulted in several club owners going bankrupt, as well as the death of the American Association and the near-capsizing of the American League.

Organized in 1885, the Brotherhood was designed to be a benevolent and protective organization for the players.

Oddly enough, it was founded by baseball writer Billy Voltz, who was also a manager of a Minor League team.

Every player was asked to contribute five dollars each month to a fund that would be available to the needy.

The Brotherhood took on a more formal tone at a meeting on October 22, 1885, organized by members of the National League's New York team. They signed the following preamble:

"We, the undersigned professional baseball players, recognizing the importance of united effort and impressed with the necessity in our behalf, do form ourselves this day into an organization to be known as the 'Brotherhood of Professional Baseball Players.' The objects we seek to accomplish are:

To protect and benefit ourselves collectively and individually.

To promote a high standard of professional conduct.

To foster and encourage the interests of the game of baseball."

The members selected John Montgomery Ward as president and Tim Keefe as secretary. The other original members of the organization included Joe Gerhardt, Buck Ewing, Roger Connor, Danny Richardson, Mickey Welch, Mike Dorgan, and Jim O'Rourke.

During the 1886 season, Ward began to organize chapters in other National League cities. The first to join was Detroit, which soon was followed by Chicago, Kansas City, Boston, Philadelphia, and Washington.

By this time, most of the prominent players in the League had entered the ranks.

Although the Brotherhood was not designed to fight club owners, most meetings consisted of little more than a debate on anti-management grievances, of which there were many.

What the players initially demanded was recognition. Ward, Ned Hanlon, and Dan Brothers formed a committee and attended the National League meeting in 1887.

A former player, Al Spalding, convinced his fellow baseball magnates that they should listen to the complaints.

When an objection was made to the reserve clause, Ward's committee was told to devise a better system of running the game.

Ward admitted that this could not be done, and the case was closed.

A year later, Spalding organized baseball's first world tour. He took his Chicago team and an All-Star club of National League opponents on a journey that began in Chicago on October

20, 1888, and included stops for exhibition games at San Francisco, Honolulu, Sydney, Melbourne, Colombo, Cairo, Naples, Rome, Paris, London, and many other cities.

The teams returned to New York just before the opening of the 1889 season, ending the tour with a mammoth banquet at Delmonico's Restaurant, at which A.G. Mills presided, and which was attended by such celebrities as Mark Twain and Theodore Roosevelt.

Here, the players learned that during their absence, John T. Brush, a new power in the league and president of the Indianapolis team, had managed to secure approval of an absurd salary-classification plan.

The players of the league were to be graded into classes from A to E, with salaries that ranged from $1,500 to $2,500.

The players realized that they were helpless to do anything about it before the 1889 season began. They insisted on an immediate hearing, but the league refused, and Ward, who had been one of the Spalding tourists, suggested a stronger response.

"There remained nothing else for the players to do, but begin organizing on a new basis," said Ward.

A meeting was held of the various Brotherhood chapters' representatives at the Fifth Avenue Hotel in New York on July 14, 1889.

Each representative was instructed to find the necessary capital in his own city and report back at an early date. The reports were all encouraging.

Men were found willing to advance the necessary funds to launch a new league and were even willing to put in capital without any return whatsoever, out of sheer love for the sport.

The players announced their intention of withdrawing from the National League on November 6, 1889, and although little more than five months remained before the new season was to begin, the Brotherhood was able to build parks in eight cities and field sufficient teams for the 1890 campaign.

The league, which came to be called both the "Brotherhood League" and the "Players League," included teams from Boston, Brooklyn, New York, Chicago, Philadelphia, Pittsburgh, Cleveland, and Buffalo.

The warring leagues adopted conflicting schedules, lied about their attendance, spread false rumors, and battled for patronage.

The real estate operators and utility magnates who had backed the Brotherhood League soon lost their early enthusiasm.

Meanwhile, the National League owner whom the players least wanted to hurt, John B. Day of the New York Giants, was ruined for life.

The Brotherhood players begged him to come to the outlaw league with them, but he remained loyal to the National League.

Loans kept him afloat for a while, but he finally surrendered his franchise to new ownership. For a time, Day managed the Giants on the field for a nominal salary, then eventually a pensioner.

Day had been offered $25,000 a year and 50 percent of the New York team's stock to act as president of the Brotherhood.

After the 1890 season, the Brotherhood beseeched the National League for a truce. Spalding informed the players that his terms were unconditional surrender.

To Spalding's astonishment, the players, unaware that the National League also was suffering terrible losses, immediately agreed, and the war was over.

19 | THE 1942 ST. LOUIS CARDINALS— GREATEST TEAM EVER?

How does one define *greatness* in a Major League Baseball team?

Definitions vary by decades and the very "experts" who render such decisions.

But when it comes to a single arbiter to produce *the* one team that stands above all, one logically would want to consult someone who witnessed more of Major League Baseball than any other human being.

That person would be Connie Mack, who began his Major League Baseball career as a player in 1886 and later ran the Philadelphia Athletics for half a century before retiring in 1951.

Mack witnessed all of the Major League dynasties, from the New York Giants of John McGraw, to the Babe Ruth-Yankees championship squads. But after the St. Louis Cardinals beat the Yankees in a five-game World Series in the autumn of 1942, Mack declared, "That St. Louis club is the greatest club I've ever seen."

How come?

"They played the game the way it ought to be played," Mack reasoned. "They took advantage of everything and didn't give anything."

Upon closer scrutiny, Mack's words make sense because this outfit–dubbed "The St. Louis Swifties" by *New York*

World-Telegram sports cartoonist Willard Mullin—did so many things well, beginning with a remarkable homestretch drive.

In fact, baseball historian Howard Siner singled out one outstanding aspect of that Cardinals team in his book *Sweet Seasons: Baseball's Top Teams Since 1920.*

"That St. Louis club," noted Siner, "staged the greatest pennant drive of all-time. On the way to the National League flag, St. Louis, steady and relentless, won 43 of its last 51 games—through the stretch they had a winning rate of .843. The Cardinals clinched the pennant on the final day of the season, beating the runner up Dodgers in five of the last six games between the clubs."

To do so, the Cardinals had to climb from being nine-and-one-half games behind Brooklyn on August 16, 1942. It didn't hurt that they even had a team fight song: "Pass the Biscuits, Mirandy." The Cards' colorful trainer, Doc Weaver, would sing the ditty in the clubhouse to loosen up the lads. And while it wasn't the biggest gap that a pennant winner had ever closed late in the season, never did any club come from behind with such a high winning rate through so much of the pulsating homestretch.

"We won it the hard way," concluded St. Louis manager Billy Southworth, "and no one won it for us. We went out and won it ourselves."

Before getting to the manner in which the Southworth-managed Cardinals dethroned the Yankees, it should be noted that winning the pennant came during a spate of incredible events, one of which featured Dodgers boss Larry MacPhail actually *declaring to his player that they would miss the pennant, even when the Dodgers still held an eight-game lead over St. Louis in mid-August.*

In fact, MacPhail made no bones about it. After studying the Cardinals carefully, he called his players together before all the New York newspapermen covering the team and said that St. Louis would beat Brooklyn in the end. Despite the Dodgers' significant lead, MacPhail unequivocally declared that they would *not* win the pennant.

"You're not hustling," said MacPhail while the media horde took copious notes. "You should be *twenty* games in front of the Cardinals, instead of only eight."

Brooklyn veteran Dixie Walker was so incensed he shouted at his boss, "I'll bet we will!" He then waved his money and challenged MacPhail before the newspapermen.

Although MacPhail backed off—just a little bit—everyone sensed that something was wrong with Larry's Dodgers. So did Branch Rickey, who ran the Cardinals at that time. Rickey also conferred with the press and was as certain about his St. Louis club going all the way as MacPhail had his doubts about his team.

"This team of mine is playing great ball, now that it has jelled," said Rickey. "I don't know about the Dodgers. But I do know that *we* will go on winning right down to the finish line. If the Dodgers stub their toes, it will be too bad for them. The Dodgers are going down and we're going up. This Cardinal club will win the pennant next year with ease, and the year after that, too."

Youth and speed were among the key ingredients for the rampaging Cardinals, whose oldest player was thirty-year-old center fielder Terry Moore, who was the captain and the one whom the players most respected, other than manager Billy Southworth.

"Billy was good for us," said Stan (The Man) Musial, then a rookie left fielder. "He knew how to handle both the rookies and veterans very well. He played good fundamental baseball, but daring. We took our chances on the base paths. First, second, third, and home. We won a lot of games, late. We came from behind in the seventh, eighth, and ninth innings. I guess we were too young to feel the pressure. That was a nice feeling."

Surrounding Moore was such promising young talent as Enos Slaughter in right field, Marty Marion at shortstop, Whitey Kurowski at third, and Walker Cooper behind the plate. Southworth's pitching staff featured Walker Cooper's brother, Mort, who went 22–7 with an astonishing 1.77 earned run average. Not to mention rookie Johnny Beazley, regarded by some analysts as the best first-year pitcher in the National League since Grover Cleveland Alexander in 1911.

Beazley boasted a 21–6 mark and a 2.14 ERA. A lefty named Max Lanier came on strong (13–8, 2.96), but was especially effective against Brooklyn (5–2) when it most counted.

Musial: "We played tough. We battled all of the clubs, especially the Dodgers. They'd knock us down, we'd knock them down. They would take somebody out at second base. It was tit for tat. That was part of the game. We didn't make many mistakes in 1942, but the best thing we had was that spirit among all of us. We just felt like we were unbeatable. We played together and spent a lot of time together. We had a great spirit on that team.

"For a great baseball team, everything just fits together. Some teams just don't fit properly; our team did. And we were close to one another. We had good pitching and a lot of speed. We were hard line drive hitters. And we were daring. That 1942 team was the best team that I ever played for and deserved to be ranked among the all-time best."

The race to the National League was amazingly close, and on September 12, the Cards finally tied the Dodgers for first place. To actually win the pennant, they beat the Dodgers in five of the last six games between them. St. Louis finished 106–48 (.688), while Brooklyn went 104–50 (.675). Southworth's St. Louis Swifties won eleven of its final dozen games, including the last seven in a row. The Dodgers won ten of its final twelve contests, finishing with eight straight wins. The Cards won the pennant on the final day of the 1942 campaign.

"Not since the old dead-ball era had a pennant winner and the number two team each won more than 100 games," noted Siner. "Never during the modern years have two stronger clubs battled so fiercely, all season long."

That, however, was only Part One of the astonishing Cardinals saga. Up next were the awe-inspiring defending World Series champion Yankees. Few experts gave the Cardinals a chance against a New York ball club that had won five world championships in six years. Odds makers called the Yankees—paced by Joe DiMaggio, Joe Gordon, and Charlie Keller, among other notables—2–1 favorites to make it six Series wins in seven years.

Southworth was unmoved by the odds. "They'll have to beat us out on the field," said the St. Louis skipper, "not in the newspaper columns. And I don't think they will beat us on the field."

For a time, in Game One it appeared as if Southworth merely was blowing St. Louis propaganda smoke. Red Ruffing was starting on the mound for New York. He had a no-hitter going until the eighth inning, at a quiet Sportsman's Park. With the Yankees-leading 7–0 in the ninth inning and with Ruffing just one pitch away from a two-hit shutout, the game appeared to be in the bag.

Suddenly, the Cards rallied and brought the score to 7–4 with the bases loaded, two out, and Musial at the plate. But Stan the Man grounded out to first, and that was that. Those who knew the Bombers best figured that a four-game sweep was entirely possible. Those who knew the Cards—starting with Musial and Southworth—figured differently.

"We had played the Yanks down in spring training that year," Musial remembered. "We had a five- or six-game series and beat the Yankees in that series. We felt that we could compete against them."

That ninth inning just-short rally infused the Cardinals with confidence. That positive feeling was shared by Branch Rickey, who sensed that the Series would turn in the Cardinals' favor, and had reasons to support his optimism. "Usually with a team so young in years and baseball experience," Rickey explained, "you see three or four men go to pot under stress. That has not happened with Southworth's team, which is a great tribute to him. If the Cards keep their feet on the ground and play the kind of ball they played all season, they can win."

And, sure enough, they did. Johnny Beazley pitched them to a 4–3 win in Game Two. Ernie White followed that with a 2–0 blanking of the Bombers—the first time the Yankees had been shut out in the World Series since 1926, against the Cardinals. Next, the St. Louis bats did the work for a 9–6 rout in Game Five, putting the Swifties only one game away from the Series clincher.

Back at Yankee Stadium for Game Five, the Bombers traded run for run into the ninth inning with the score tied at two apiece. But in the top of the ninth, Cards third baseman Whitey Kurowski broke the Bronx men with a two-run homer, while Beazley took his second victory of the Series.

The scene in the winner's clubhouse was right out of a Hollywood movie. When aging Baseball Commissioner Kenesaw Mountain Landis entered the dressing room, the Cards lifted the distinguished jurist to the ceiling. Ditto for boss Branch Rickey, followed by Series-clinching hero Kurowski, who then had his uniform torn to pieces.

Not that Kurowski would mind it a bit, because he was still smiling from ear to ear, while Doc Weaver led them through one more chorus of "Pass the Biscuits, Mirandy."

Connie Mack called those Cardinals the greatest team he has ever seen, and Stan Musial indicated what put them in that ethereal position.

"We had the right spirit and love of the game," the Man explained. "You have to have courage and talent, and work hard. A lot has to do with intangibles, like confidence. In the homestretch, we wanted to keep going and try to repeat the victories. To get a group like that together is hard to do, but it only happens every once in a while."

But never better than in that season of 1942.

20 | WORST BOOING OF A PRESIDENT AT A BASEBALL GAME

Ironically, **these days** at sporting events often are marked by the booing of sports leaders. For example, in hockey just about any time Commissioner Gary Bettman makes a public appearance, he can expect to receive the Bronx cheers.

Just when this form of insolence began is debatable, but one baseball episode often is cited as the moment when decorum for high officials went out the window.

It happened on October 6, 1931, during the presidency of Herbert Hoover, who happened to attend Game Three of the World Series in Philadelphia between the St. Louis Cardinals and Philadelphia Athletics.

Hoover, a Republican, had been elected president in 1929 and was the man generally held responsible for the Great Depression, which had blanketed the nation. Nevertheless, it had been traditional for audiences, no matter how unhappy, to greet the presidential party with reverence and applause at sporting events such as the World Series.

When Hoover arrived, there was a perfunctory pattering of palms behind the dugouts, whereupon Hoover waved his hat and smiled. But as the president approached his official box, someone booed. Then came another hoot, and another. Joe Williams, who covered the World Series for the *New York World-Telegram*, recalled how quickly the decibel count multiplied. "Soon," said Williams, "it seemed that almost everyone in the park was booing."

Prohibition was still in vogue, and the crowd, en masse, seemed to realize that Hoover had lined up on the side of the drys, supporting the Prohibition law. Suddenly, the boos changed to a deafening chant: "We want beer. We want beer!"

As soon as the first inning was underway, the crowd's attention was distracted from the Hoovers to the Cardinals and Athletics. However, at the end of the eighth inning, a voice boomed over the ballpark loudspeaker. "Silence. Silence, please." Hoover and his party were ready to leave the game. The public address announcer pleaded for the courtesy and asked everyone in the stadium to remain seated.

The plea was ignored. Hoover, holding his wife by the arm, walked past the Athletics' dugout amid a cacophony of boos, followed by an equally deafening chant: "We want beer! We want beer!"

Hoover later explained that he walked out before the game's end because he had received two telegrams; one told of the death of a personal friend and the other revealed that the United States had gone off the gold standard. "Under the circumstances," said Hoover, "I decided I had no business watching a ball game." Despite hostile reaction at the World Series game, Hoover continued to attend baseball games at various stadia in later years.

II
Fascinating Characters

21 | BABE RUTH AS PITCHING STAR AND CAR-BATTERING ACE

Renowned as "the Sultan of Swat" for his prodigious home runs, Babe Ruth also was an ace on the mound. Many baseball historians insist that the man known as El Bambino could have remained a star pitcher—and future Hall of Famer because of that—without having to move into the outfield. How good was he as a twirler? Try this one on for size:

Once, the Babe tossed twenty-nine and two-thirds consecutive scoreless innings during *World Series games*.

Part of Ruth's success was his control, which was more than could be said when he was behind the wheel of a car. Once, the Babe's chroniclers noted, "Many a day the morning papers carried headlines about yet another custom-built car that Ruth had wrapped around a lamp post."

22 | THE MOST INCREDIBLE WORLD SERIES ALIBI

Like other athletes, baseball players hate to lose.

Sometimes—as in the World Series, for example—losing is more painful than it is for a regular season game.

That might explain how Billy Loes uttered the most absurd rationale after blowing a World Series game to the New York Yankees. The lean Lanky Loes was admired for his droll, and occasionally bizarre, humor. His most widely played retort was delivered during the 1952 World Series when he mistook the velocity of a grounder to the mound and erred on the play. Questioned about the error, Loes replied with a straight face: "I lost it in the sun!"

A lesser but philosophically better line was delivered in Loes' career. Many observers wondered why a pitcher with so much natural talent could continually fail to win more than fourteen games a season, even though he was backed by a strong club. When a reporter questioned Loes about his perennial failure to reach the twenty-win plateau, Billy mulled over the query for a moment and then rather candidly commented that such a Promethean effort would be damaging to his psyche: "If you win twenty," said Loes, "they want you to do it every year."

23 | A YANKEES BATBOY WAS FIRED FOR ALMOST KILLING BABE RUTH—AND LATER BECAME A FILM STAR

If these episodes didn't actually happen, you might believe that a Hollywood scriptwriter made them up. Come to think of it, Hollywood is partially involved in this remarkable bit of baseball trivia.

When Babe Ruth was at the apex of his career, a robust young batboy worshipped "the Sultan of Swat," and the Babe, in return, encouraged the young man to pursue a baseball career. The batboy in question was none other than William Bendix, and Babe's very wish was Bendix's command: the kid would shine the Babe's shoes, run his errands, and provide Ruth with all the food the heavy-eating Babe would require.

One day before a game, Ruth dispatched Bendix to obtain some soda pop and hot dogs. Dutifully, the kid returned with a dozen frankfurters and several quarts of soda. As usual, Ruth, one of sportdom's notorious trenchermen, devoured everything that Bendix delivered to the locker room.

This time the feast took its toll and, later in the afternoon, Ruth collapsed with severe stomach pains and was rushed to the hospital. Headlines across the country proclaimed that Ruth actually was dying. When the Yankees' front office discovered that

William Bendix had delivered the food to Ruth, the young batboy was summarily dismissed.

The Babe recovered and continued hitting home runs and drawing fans to every ballpark in the American League. Meanwhile, the brokenhearted Bendix abandoned his pursuit of a baseball career and, instead, turned to the theater.

Curiously, Bendix played hundreds of roles, many of them involving sports figures. One of his popular parts was that of "The Bambino" himself, in *The Babe Ruth Story*.

24 | DOUBLE DUTY WAS HIS NAME; CATCHING AND PITCHING IN A DOUBLEHEADER WAS HIS CLAIM TO FAME

The Pittsburgh Crawfords of the Negro National League certainly got their money's worth from Ted Radcliffe.

To begin, Radcliffe was behind the plate for nine innings as the Crawfords went 5–0 in the first game of a double-header at Yankee Stadium.

In the second game, Ted took the mound and spun a 4–0 shut-out. Talk about double dipping. As a result, Radcliffe earned the nickname "Double Duty," thanks to journalist Damon Runyon.

After seeing Radcliffe perform, Runyon wrote, "It was worth the admission price of two to see Double Duty out there in action."

Those who played with and against Radcliffe toasted his versatility. "He never got the recognition he should have," said shortstop Jake Stephens. "In my book, he was one of the greatest."

Added Catcher Royal "Skink" Browning: "Radcliffe could catch the first game, pitch the second–and was a terror at both of them."

25 | TWO BROTHERS WHO AMASSED AN ASTONISHING WIN TOTAL

Baseball has been happily filled with amazing brother acts. For example, the Cardinals won multiple World Series with Mort Cooper on the mound and his brother Walker behind the plate.

And earlier, Redbirds teams featured a pair of sterling pitchers, the brothers Dizzy and Daffy Dean.

But when it came to victories, the Deans took a backseat to Gaylord and Jim Perry. Between them, they accumulated an amazing 529 victories.

The runners-up were the Mathewsons, Christy and Henry, who registered their second-place total of 373 while with the New York Giants in the early 1900s. There's just one catch with the Mathewson brothers: Christy won all of those games! Henry Mathewson pitched for the Giants in 1906 and 1907, appeared in three games, and had one decision—a loss. Not much of a contributor.

The Perry brothers had a much more equitable distribution of wins. Jim had 215 wins, while younger brother Gaylord earned 314 wins. They did get the chance to play together for the Cleveland Indians in 1974 and 1975.

26 | THE BEST PUT-DOWN OF AN AMERICAN PRESIDENT BY A BASEBALL STAR

Normally, the president of the United States—no matter what the decade, nor political affiliation—is treated with the upmost respect by ballplayers. But when someone with the stature and humor of a Babe Ruth is concerned, all bets are off.

One president who made the discovery was the Republican Herbert Hoover.

The first year of the Great Depression, Ruth signed a contract for $80,000. The Yankees had rewarded him with the then-astronomical salary because of his popularity as a slugger and value to the team at the box office. Still, $80,000 was more than a lot of money; it was outrageous at that time.

At least that was the opinion of one sportswriter, who asked Ruth how it felt to earn more money than the president of the United States. Ruth, the inimitable Bambino, mulled over the question, realized how unpopular the president had become in those Depression days, and then shot back: "Well, I had a better year than he did!"

27 | FROM PRISON TO THE MAJORS— THANKS TO BILLY MARTIN

n old song, "If I Had The Wings Of An Angel–Over These Prison Walls I Would Fly," depicts a fantasizing convict musing about his potential escape from the penitentiary.

It's hard to determine whether Ron LeFlore had that tune in mind while an inmate in the Jackson State Prison.

Incarcerated on a five-to-fifteen-year sentence for armed robbery, LeFlore volunteered to play for the prison baseball team. In time, he became so good that fellow inmate, Jim Karella, began promoting LeFlore as a potential pro ballplayer.

That was the start of Ron's good fortune. It multiplied when then Detroit Tigers manager Billy Martin visited Jackson State and began hearing—over and over and over again—about LeFore's diamond talent.

As a result, the Tigers arranged for LeFlore's furlough and a tryout at Tiger Stadium. It was more of a good will gesture than anything else.

But LeFlore surprised even the skeptics, and the Tigers signed him to a Minor League contract on July 2, 1973, the day he was paroled.

After playing less than one season in the minors, LeFlore was called up by the Tigers in 1974. He became a star for his hometown team, a plus-.300 hitter, and a mainstay on a young and aggressive team.

LeFlore's story sounds good enough for a Hollywood scriptwriter, doesn't it? Well, CBS-TV thought so and produced *One in a Million*, Ron's life story starring LeVar Burton of *Roots* fame, as LeFlore.

Billy Martin was played by—who else?—Billy Martin. Said Burton of Martin: "He follows instructions like a little leaguer at tryouts. You know, Billy's a pussycat, really. A pussycat with chutzpah."

28 | THE INCREDIBLE STORY OF A TEENAGE VENDOR WHO LATER RETURNED TO THE SAME FIELD AS A BIG LEAGUE PLAYER

Eddie Glynn lived less than two miles from Shea Stadium when the ballpark opened in 1964. In 1967, he began working at the stadium as a vendor later. He would later return to play in the World Series as a member of the 1979 Mets.

Glynn recalled, "I wasn't into the vendor tricks, like tossing peanuts and catching coins." He was more intent on studying the styles of the various players.

In 1972, Glynn signed with the Detroit Tigers organization. He was traded to the Mets in 1979 for pitcher Mardie Cornejo.

Upon his return to Shea, Glynn remarked, "It was like a dream come true. I'd go around talking to the vendors and fans after the game. But it worked the other way, too. If I had a bad game, the fans would get on me. 'Hey, Glynn, go back to selling hot dogs.'"

In May 1980, the Mets held a Hot Dog day and gave Glynn a hot dog vending tray with his number, 48, embossed on the side. Glynn responded by climbing into the stands and hawking hot dogs.

29 | MICKEY MANTLE AND ROGER MARIS AS MOVIE STARS—IT HAPPENED IN HOLLYWOOD

The Yankees sluggers were so popular in the early 1960s that film moguls decided to make actors out of them, at least for one film.

It's called *Safe at Home* (1962) and is about a Little Leaguer. Simply put, the plot has the lad running away from home to the Yankees spring training camp, where he asks the outfield starters to appear at a Little League banquet.

30 | ROOKIE MANAGERS ARE NOT SUPPOSED TO BE PENNANT- AND WORLD SERIES-WINNERS RIGHT OFF THE BAT

Most successful baseball skippers will tell you that it takes a few seasons to acclimatize to the nuances of managing, and some never do.

But Bill Terry and Frankie Frisch were incredible exceptions to the rule.

What the pair accomplished in 1933 and 1934 really was one for the books, and a lesson from the proverb *nothing ventured, nothing gained.*

Their feat was winning both the pennant *and* the World Series in their first full seasons as managers.

Terry led the New York Giants to the 1933 World Series against the Washington Senators, who were managed by Joe Cronin, himself a first-year manager.

In 1934, Frisch's St. Louis Cardinals took the crown by defeating the Detroit Tigers, whose manager, Mickey Cochrane, also happened to be a first-year leader.

Other members of the Hall of Fame to win pennants in their first full year of managing were: Tris Speaker, Cleveland Indians, 1920; Rogers Hornsby, St. Louis Cardinals, 1926; and Yogi Berra, New York Yankees, 1964.

Speaker, Hornsby, and Frisch never won another pennant. Cochrane and the Tigers won the pennant in 1935 and went on to defeat the Chicago Cubs in the World Series.

Cronin managed for eleven fruitless years before winning another pennant with the Boston Red Sox in 1946. Berra won the National League Championship in 1973 at the New York Mets' helm.

31 | A BATTER WHO STRUCK OUT ON ONLY TWO STRIKES

Ray Chapman was a pretty good ballplayer and not a bad hitter at that. But when it came to facing Walter Johnson, he might as well have been a piece of tissue paper. As for Johnson, his pitching strategy was simple and straightforward.

He relied on his fastball. If it failed to work the first time, he'd throw a faster one the next time. Batters often excuse their strikeouts by explaining, "How can you hit 'em if you can't see 'em?"

One time, Ray Chapman faced the unhittable Johnson. After two swinging strikes, Chapman walked out of the batter's box and headed for the dugout in disgust.

"Wait a minute," the umpire called after him, "you've got another strike coming."

"Never mind," replied Chapman, "I don't want it."

32 | ALMOST GIVEN UP FOR DEAD IN WORLD WAR II, LOU BRISSIE RETURNED TO PITCH IN THE MAJORS

Before the Japanese sneak attack on Pearl Harbor, December 7, 1941, Lou Brissie was playing collegiate baseball and was scouted by the Philadelphia Athletics. The A's boss, Connie Mack, was impressed with Brissie, but did not want to take him right away. Mack advised Brissie to go to college first and then return to Philadelphia. He added that there would be a uniform waiting for him. Mack even helped Brissie with college expenses to show the young man how serious he was about the boy's future. Brissie, in turn, was determined to keep Mack's faith in him and continued playing in college.

A year after the bombing of Pearl Harbor, Brissie felt he could no longer put off enlisting. He told his college coach, Coach McNair, of his decision. Coach McNair did not try to dissuade the boy. He knew the boy was strong-willed and his efforts would be in vain.

Two years later, on December 7, 1944, Corporal Brissie and his infantry were in the Appenine Mountains outside of Bologna, Italy. German attackers shelled his platoon. Brissie and his entire outfit were hit. Most of the men were killed, the others critically wounded. Brissie was one of the more fortunate; nevertheless, he was badly wounded. He lay in mud until a search party arrived.

To Brissie's dismay, they appeared to be leaving him there, assuming that all of the men had been killed. Brissie tried to call out to them but could not, due to shock. Then, one of the men in the search party noticed Brissie move. Brissie was given medical attention at a nearby aid station. Forty transfusions later, Brissie was transferred to the evacuation hospital in Naples.

One morning, Brissie awoke to find a doctor leaning over him. The doctor turned to an aide and said, "This leg will have to come off." Brissie was stunned. He mustered all the strength he could and pleaded with the doctor not to amputate his leg. "I'm a baseball player, and I've got to play ball," Brissie explained. Fortunately for Brissie, the doctor was a baseball fan and understood Brissie's plight. The boy's strong will to keep his leg encouraged the doctor to agree that he would do everything he could to save it for him.

Brissie's leg had been completely shattered. There was scarcely a piece of bone in his leg that was left intact. The doctor did everything he could to put Brissie's leg back together. Brissie underwent many complicated operations at various hospitals around the country and around the world.

Connie Mack had written Brissie through his years in the army, and after the boy was shot, wrote him more often. Connie assured Lou that there would still be a uniform waiting for him upon his release from the army.

One morning in July 1949, Lou Brissie walked up to Connie Mack's office on a crutch. Just as Connie had promised, Lou's uniform was ready for him. Brissie wore the uniform and even warmed up with the bullpen catcher. But the idea that he would ever play Major League Baseball still seemed far-fetched. Brissie underwent major surgery a few days later for an infection in his leg. Most of the Athletics thought they had seen the last of Lou Brissie.

Lou Brissie showed up at spring training in Florida the next year, much to the surprise of the other players. Although not as agile as most, Brissie still managed to play ball. Only one year later, Brissie was pitching for the Philadelphia Athletics. By the end of his career, Brissie had pitched six full seasons of Major League ball.

33 | SIX MANAGERS IN FOUR YEARS— ONLY STEINBRENNER COULD DO IT

During **George Steinbrenner's** reign as the boss of the New York Yankees, the Stadium was dubbed "The Bronx Zoo" for a reason: George ran a managerial merry-go-round, rare in baseball history.

The Boss started making wholesale changes in 1980, when he replaced Billy Martin, on his second tour as manager, with Dick Howser.

Howser was a good choice; he motivated his players (including moody Reggie Jackson) and won the division title. Jackson enjoyed his best season ever: forty-one homers and a .300 average. Jackson's homers tied for the league lead with Ben Oglivie.

But Howser's Yankees collapsed in the playoffs, losing in three games straight to the Kansas City Royals. Infuriated, Steinbrenner replaced Howser with Gene Michael, the team's general manager.

Michael's cautious managing and deference to George Steinbrenner kept him in first place and in charge when the strike hit in 1981. After the strike, the Yankees were declared the "first-half" winners, assured of a playoff berth. But his over cautious managing in the second half lost games and alienated him from the players. Steinbrenner decided to change managers, bringing in

Bob Lemon, who had managed the Yankees' great World Championship team in 1978.

Lemon stabilized the team and guided it to a victory in the playoffs. But in the World Series, after the Yanks won the first two games, the Dodgers came back to win four in a row. Pitcher George Frazier lost three games for the Yanks in the Series, setting a new World Series record.

Even so, Steinbrenner promised Lemon that he could manage the Yankees all the way through the '82 season, and Lemon returned to open it. But the Yankees fell apart quickly without Reggie Jackson, who had fled to the Angels after a disastrous 1981 season.

Bereft of effective power and pitching, the Yankees stumbled around until mid-May, when Steinbrenner had seen enough. Out went Lemon; back came Gene Michael.

However, Michael was no improvement. One night, the Yankees lost both ends of a doubleheader to the lowly Cleveland Indians, with Steinbrenner in attendance. The fans directed their wrath at Steinbrenner, and the boss was annoyed. His first move was to allow fans to use their tickets as rain checks for other games.

His second move was to fire Gene Michael and bring in super scout and former pitching coach Clyde King as manager. King restored some order, but the season was too far gone to save.

When all was over, Steinbrenner changed managers again, bringing in his sixth skipper, on his third trip: Billy Martin, the very man he started with at the end of 1979.

Round and round goes the merry-go-round.

34 | THE IMPROBABLE COMEBACK IN THE SUMMER OF 1978

The 1978 Yankee season was a story written for Hollywood. The turbulent relationship between Reggie Jackson and manager Billy Martin was a story in itself.

It's hard to imagine, after winning the World Series in 1977, that the Yankees would repeat without their manager. That's exactly what happened in 1978.

After Martin learned about Yankees principal owner George Steinbrenner's plan to fire him, he lashed out to the public. "They deserve each other. One's a born liar [Reggie Jackson] and the other's convicted [referring to Steinbrenner's conviction for making illegal donations to Richard Nixon's 1972 campaign]."

The next day, on July 24, Martin resigned before George could fire him. The Yankees hired Bob Lemon, who was fired approximately one month earlier by the Chicago White Sox.

The Red Sox were running away with the American League East. Lemon's team gave New York three months of baseball that you had to see to believe. The Yankees were ten and a half games out of the lead.

Lemon first addressed the team by saying, "So why don't you just go out and play the way you did last year, and I'll try to stay the hell out of the way?"

Lemon's objectives were clear: straighten out the pitching staff and get Jackson to play up to his ability.

The Yankees went on a tear, winning almost every time they played. The Yankees somehow put themselves within striking distance of the Boston Red Sox, with four games left, all against the Red Sox, and all in Fenway Park. This series went on to be known as the Boston Massacre.

After sweeping all four games, the teams played a one-game playoff to determine who would be going to the postseason.

The playoff game had a similar trajectory to that of the season. The Red Sox jumped out to an early lead, and the Yankees battled their way back.

The most unlikely of players became a name that will forever live in infamy. Bucky Dent hit a towering drive over the Green Monster to give the Yankees a 3–2 lead.

The Yankees went on to win the game and the World Series for a second consecutive season.

What many fail to remember is that these two teams battled through perhaps the finest division in baseball history—five teams finished with at least eighty-six wins, four of them with ninety wins or more. That the Yankees passed all of them in their run, and then won on enemy turf with a home run from their choked-up shortstop, all before winning a second straight World Series crown, makes this the cream of the crop in terms of comebacks in the American League.

35 | FROM THIRD-STRING CATCHER TO FIRST-STRING SPY

Morris (Moe) Berg hardly had a distinguished baseball career. If anything, his only claim to diamond fame was longevity. The catcher from Newark, NJ, lasted in the bigs from 1923 to 1939, playing for the Brooklyn Dodgers, Chicago White Sox, Cleveland Indians, Washington Senators, and finally, the Boston Red Sox.

It was in the realm of spying that Berg was exceptionally successful. Working for Uncle Sam when he wasn't behind the plate—among other feats—Berg laid the groundwork for General Jimmy Doolittle's thirty-second bombing of Tokyo in 1942.

In another instance, Berg was responsible for British Prime Minister Winston Churchill's support of Marshal Josip Broz Tito's Nazi-resistance group over Commander Dragoljub Mihalovic's Serbian forces. Parachuting into Yugoslavia at age forty-one, Berg took stock of Marshal Tito's scrappy partisans and reported back to Churchill.

It was Moe's impressive status as a polyglot that led him to espionage. His pharmacist father, Bernard, taught him Hebrew and Yiddish, and he learned Latin, Greek, and French in high school. At Princeton University, Berg added Spanish, Italian, German, and Sanskrit to his repertoire, and after studying in Paris and then Columbia Law School, he picked up Hungarian, Portuguese, Arabic, Japanese, Korean, Chinese languages, and more Indian languages. In all, he boasted knowledge of fifteen languages, not to mention the various regional dialects.

Berg began playing baseball at age four, but his stern father disapproved of the ball game and refused to watch his son play, even when Moe played shortstop for Princeton. After college, Berg went on to play for the Brooklyn Robins (later the Dodgers) as a backup catcher. His baseball career was mediocre at best, but he was venerated by sportswriters, fellow players, and fans alike for his intellectual brilliance.

Japanese baseball fans were no exception; they were thrilled when Berg was, somewhat unexpectedly and, in light of his position as a third-string catcher, somewhat undeservedly, chosen to accompany MLB greats, such as Babe Ruth and Lou Gehrig, on an All-Star tour of Japan in 1934. Yet, unbeknownst to all—save for key U.S. government officials—Berg was not on tour to promote the sport of baseball.

Instead, the Japanese-speaking Princeton grad was instructed to film key features of Tokyo for use in General Doolittle's 1942 raid.

Berg was also tasked with determining how close the Nazis were to constructing the world's first atomic bomb. With famed physicist Werner Heisenberg at the forefront of the German nuclear energy project, the stakes were getting higher by the day.

Posing as a Swiss graduate student, Moe Berg sat in the front row of the Nobel Laureate's lecture with a pistol and a cyanide pill in his pocket. His task: assess the Nazi's progress on building a nuclear bomb, and if he judged that they were close to achieving their goal, he was to shoot Heisenberg and swallow the cyanide pill. Fortunately for all, Berg's assessment came back negative.

After the war, Berg found himself out of a job. He occasionally received intelligence assignments, but always saw himself as a ballplayer. When asked, "Why are you wasting your talent?" Berg responded, "I'd rather be a ballplayer than a Justice on the U.S. Supreme Court."

Moe Berg was awarded the Medal of Merit—America's highest honor for a civilian in wartime. But Berg refused to accept it, as he could not tell people about his exploits. After his death, his sister accepted the medal, and it hangs in the Baseball Hall of Fame, in Cooperstown, NY.

36 | STAN MUSIAL SHOWS WHY HE IS "THE MAN"

When Stan Musial's name comes up for discussion among those who know baseball's history best, the first of his feats that comes to mind is the man's seven National League batting championships.

His clutch hitting—especially at Brooklyn's Ebbets Field—inspired Dodger fans to nickname him "the Man."

More specifically, when Musial walked up to the batter's box at the Flatbush ballpark, Dodger fans were likely to murmur, "Here comes the man!" A writer covering the Dodgers-Cardinals game one day overheard the comment, and from that point on, Musial was "Stan the Man."

As effective as Musial was in Brooklyn, his best day as a home run hitter took place on May 2, 1954, at Busch Stadium in St. Louis. On that day, in a doubleheader against the New York Giants, Musial hit five home runs.

Musial had three homers in the Cards' first fourteen games, and there was little reason to suspect that he would break out in a rash of four-baggers this time, particularly with Johnny Antonelli, one of the league's top southpaws, pitching the first game for the Giants.

His third and final home run in the first game was a game-winning blow. The Cards won 10–6 behind Stan's three home run performance.

Manager Leo Durocher of the Giants nominated Don Liddle, another lefty, to work the nightcap. In Musial's second plate appearance of the second game, he was finally retired: the first time he was sent back to the dugout all day.

Knuckleballer Hoyt Wilhelm was on the mound for the Giants when Musial came to the plate again. With one man on base, Musial connected again, hammering a ball over the pavilion roof for his fourth homer of the day.

HOYT WILHELM

GIANTS

HALL OF FAME '85

Then in the seventh inning, Stan punished another ball over the right field roof. This narrowed the Giants' lead to one run. The Cards could not get another run across and split the doubleheader.

In eight official trips to the plate, Musial collected five home runs, one single, nine runs batted in, and twenty-one total bases. He set a Major League record with his five homers in the twin bill and tied the record for homers in two consecutive games.

37 | FROM MISTER ANONYMITY TO ALL-TIME HERO

For most of his baseball career, preceding the 1951 season and right up to the homestretch, Bobby Thomson of the New York Giants hardly could be called a household name in the diamond business.

True, the Jints' third baseman-outfielder played well, but hardly was a headline-grabber. But that was to change in one of the most curious homestretches in history.

By late summer, the Giants and Brooklyn Dodgers had engaged in a thrilling late-season race for the playoffs. The Giants, who trailed the League-leading Dodgers by thirteen and a half games in mid-August, managed to climb their way back. They won thirty-seven of their final forty-four games and secured the opportunity to play the Dodgers in a three-game playoff for the pennant.

In dramatic fashion, the series came down to a decisive third game. The Dodgers sent twenty-game winner Don Newcombe to the mound to face the Giants in the Polo Grounds. And he produced. Newcombe took a 4–1 lead to the ninth. The righty was dominant for eight innings, but ran out of steam to open the ninth. After giving up a run on three hits and only retiring one batter, Newcombe's day was done. Enter former twenty-one-game winner Ralph Branca.

Branca was given the task of facing the Giants' Bobby Thomson with the tying runs on base. Thomson had already done damage—both good and bad—in the series. His go-ahead two-run homer in the first game gave the Giants an early advantage in the playoff. The second game was a much different story. Thomson's base-running mistakes and errors in the field contributed to a defeat at the hands of the Dodgers. He had a chance to redeem himself against Branca.

After taking a first-pitch strike, Thomson locked in on the second one, a fastball. He pulled it to left field. When the ball entered the stands above the left field wall, the Polo Grounds erupted. Thomson triumphantly circled the bases and was welcomed at home plate by his even happier teammates.

While fewer than thirty-five thousand could say they actually saw "the shot heard 'round the world," Russ Hodges illustrated the scene for tens of thousands listening to the radio broadcast, putting them at the Polo Grounds with the spectators. Hodges' call of "the shot heard 'round the world" is one of the most memorable in sports history. The image of Thomson rounding the bases isn't complete without Hodges' "The Giants win the pennant!" call to accompany it.

38 | THE EVANGELIST WHO DOUBLED AS A BASEBALL STAR

Religion and baseball often go hand in hand, but in one extreme case, a member of the clergy also happened to be a diamond star.

In his day, Billy Sunday was more renowned as a ballplayer than he was before turning to a career on the pulpit, where his full moniker was Reverend Billy Sunday.

Before that, he was an outstanding outfielder with the Chicago White Stockings. Many observers credited Sunday with helping Chicago win the pennant in 1886. It all happened in a crucial game between Detroit and Chicago, with the White Stockings holding a slim lead over their opponents.

Detroit had two men on base with two out and catcher Charley Bennett at the plate. The pitch was just where Bennett wanted it, and he slammed the ball toward very deep right field. Sunday, who was considered the fastest man in both leagues, turned and ran in the direction of the ball. He leaped over a bench on the lip of the outfield and continued running. As he made his way, Sunday talked out loud: "Oh, God. If you're going to help me, come on now!" At this point, Sunday leaped in the air and threw up his hand. He nabbed the ball and fell on his back. Thanks to Sunday, Chicago won the game and, eventually, the pennant.

Sunday enjoyed telling friends that he played for two teams, the White Stockings and "God's team." When asked how he got on God's team, Billy would explain: "I walked down a street in Chicago with some ballplayers, and we went into a saloon. It was Sunday afternoon and we got tanked up, and then went and sat down on a curbing. Across the street, a company of men and women were playing on instruments—horns, flutes and slide trombones—and the others were singing the gospel hymns that I used to hear my mother sing back in the log cabin in Iowa and back in the old church where I used to go to Sunday school. I arose and said to the boys, 'I'm through. I am going to Jesus Christ. We've come to the parting of the ways.'"

Although his teammates needled him, Sunday followed the Salvation Army singers into the Pacific Garden Restaurant Mission on Van Buren Street. Billy may not have known it at the time, but he was on his way to the Sawdust Trail where, as he put it, he would emerge as the scrappiest antagonist that "Blazing-eyed, eleven-hoofed, forked-tail old Devil" ever had to go against.

39 | WAS THIS THE ALL-TIME BASEBALL BONEHEAD PLAY?

A **name and expression** have become synonymous in baseball lore over the decades.

The ballplayer was Fred Merkle of the New York Giants.

The expression that became so closely synonymous with the first baseman was *bonehead*.

Until that date, September 23, 1908, Merkle was as anonymous as a National League rookie could be. But that all changed in a game against the Chicago Cubs.

It was a contest that would decide the pennant, and it appeared as if the Giants would take the flag.

After all, they were nestled in first place by six percentage points over Chicago and were playing at home in Harlem.

But that was where the Giants' good luck ended and Merkle's *bonehead* saga reached Chapter One.

With the score tied, 1–1, and two out in the last half of the ninth inning, Moose McCormick of the Giants was on third and Merkle on first.

When Al Bridwell singled to center field and McCormick crossed the plate with what appeared to be the winning run, the jubilant crowd surged onto the field.

But Merkle, seeing McCormick score, had never bothered to continue to second base. Instead, he ran to the clubhouse to escape the onrushing fans.

Meanwhile, Solly Hoffman, the Cubs' center fielder, threw the ball toward second base, but his throw was wild.

Floyd Kroh, a substitute, attempted to retrieve it, but Joe McGinnity raced over from the Giants' coaching box, wrestled him for it, and is believed to have thrown it into the stands.

Somehow, the second baseman obtained another ball, stepped on second, and raced over to the plate umpire, Hank O'Day.

The first base umpire, Robert Emslie, had been watching first and missed the play entirely. But when O'Day told him what had happened, Emslie called Merkle out.

O'Day, an umpire in the league as early as 1888, went back to his hotel and after eating dinner, sat down and wrote the following letter to Harry G. Pulliam, president of the National League.

NEW YORK, SEPT. 23/08
HARRY C. PULLIAM, ESQ.
PRES. NAT. LEAGUE

Dear Sir:
In the Game today at New York between New York and Chicago, in the last half of the ninth inning the score was tied 1–1, New York was at the bat, with two men out, McCormick of New York on 3rd base and Merkle of N.Y. on 1st base; Bridwell was at bat and hit a clean single Base-Hit to center field. Merkle did not run the ball out; he started toward second base, but getting half way there he turned and ran down the field toward the clubhouse. The ball was fielded in to second base for a Chicago man to make the play, when McGinnity ran from the coacher's box out in the field to second base and interfered with the play being made. Emslie, who

said he did not watch Merkle, asked if Merkle touched second base. I said he did not. Then Emslie called Merkle out, and I would not allow McCormick's run to score. The game at the end of the ninth inning was 1–1. The people ran out on the field. I did not ask to have the field cleared, as it was too dark to continue play.
Yours Respectfully,

Henry O'Day

To understand properly the meaning of the Merkle play and to determine whether O'Day and Emslie made a good decision, some background is necessary.

The rules, of course, are quite clear that when the third out of an inning is a force-out, no runs can score on the play. The trouble was, the rule had never been enforced.

Less than three weeks earlier, on September 4, in a game between Pittsburgh and Chicago, a Pirate runner, Warren Gill, did exactly what Merkle did.

O'Day was umpiring the game and refused to call Gill out. He couldn't confer with anyone, as he was umpiring the game alone.

But after thinking about it, O'Day determined that if the play ever happened again, he would call the runner out.

So there never would have been a Merkle story if O'Day had not been the umpire behind the plate, or if the play on Gill had not come up, or if the same man, Bud Evers, had not been playing second base.

It was an unusual and coincidental set of circumstances.

Bill Klem, one of the best known of all Major League umpires, always insisted that the decision on Merkle was the worst in the history of baseball.

Klem's thinking was that the rule in question was intended to apply only to infield grounders and not to safe hits. However, O'Day interpreted the rule as written.

Both the Giants and the Cubs protested the decision of the umpires to replay the "tied" game. The Giants claimed that they had legitimately won the game, 2–1.

The Cubs maintained that they should be awarded the game by forfeit, first because of McGinnity's interference, and then because the Giants had refused to play the game the following day, as required by league rules.

Despite Pulliam's decision to side with the umpires, the two teams continued their protest to the league's board of directors, which ordered the game replayed on October 8.

The Giants and Cubs were tied for first place on the day of the replayed game, each with 98–55 records. The Cubs defeated the Giants, 4–2, and annexed the championship.

In failing to touch second base, Merkle only did what many players had already done, yet he was called every epithet printable, and some that weren't.

The Sporting Life, a baseball publication, noted that "through the inexcusable stupidity of Merkle, a substitute, the Giants had a sure victory turned into a doubtful one, a game was played in dispute, a complicated and disagreeable controversy was started, and perhaps the championship imperilled or lost."

Apparently, the only prominent sportswriter to take a sensible view of the affair was Paul W. Eaton, a freelance writer in Washington, D.C.

"A protest may well be recorded against the many severe criticisms of Merkle that have been made," Eaton wrote.

"His accusers seem to have agreed on the epithet of 'bonehead.' It can be stated most emphatically that in failing to touch second after Bridwell's hit, Merkle did only what had been done in hundreds of championship games in the Major Leagues."

Merkle, understandably heartbroken, returned to his parents' home in Toledo, Ohio. Reporters crowded around him there, swarming like bees.

Merkle then told a side of the story that had eluded everyone–that his hit that sent McCormick to third might easily have been for extra bases.

"The single that set up the play might have been a double or a triple," he explained. "But Jack Hayden, the Cub right fielder, made a wonderful stab and knocked down the drive. At that, I could have gone to second easily, but with one run needed to win and a man on third, I played it safe. When Bridwell got the single that should have won the game, I was so happy over the victory, I started for the clubhouse, figuring, of course, on getting out of the way before the crowd blocked the field. When I heard Evers calling for the ball, and noticed the excitement, I did not know at first what it was about, but the meaning of it all suddenly dawned on me and I wished that a large, roomy, and comfortable hole would open up and swallow me. But it is all over now and will have to be forgotten."

But seven years later, the play was not forgotten. At that time, a writer asked Merkle, "Do you get any fun out of baseball?"

"No," Merkle replied, "I wouldn't call it fun. I have too rough a time out there."

"Do the fans still ride you?"

"Yes. The worst thing is, I can't do things other players do without attracting attention. Little slips that would be excused in other players are burned into me by the crowds. Of course, I have made mistakes with the rest, but I have to do double duty. If any play I'm concerned with goes wrong, I'm the fellow who gets the blame, no matter where the thing went off the line. I try not to mind it too much; I've been ridden enough to get used to it, but nobody's as thick-skinned, but what a roast will get under his skin at some time or another."

The Merkle play was such a "touching" story that the following year a book called *Touching Second?* was dedicated to the second baseman, Evers, by Hughie Fullerton.

Surprisingly, there is reason to believe that Merkle did touch second. But not exactly right after the incident.

Tom Meany, a baseball authority and author, once learned after the game that Merkle's manager had seen to it that Merkle was secluded in the Shelbourne Hotel in Brighton Beach, Brooklyn, and that in the middle of the night he had the boy return to the Polo Grounds and touch second, so that if he were ever asked under oath, he could swear that on September 23, 1908, he had second!

40 | BARNEY KREMENKO'S MISTAKEN SIGNALS

D uring the late 1940s and early 1950s, Barney Kremenko covered the New York Giants for the *Journal*, Hearst's flagship afternoon daily in New York City.

As sports journalists go, Kremenko was passionate in the extreme. He loved the Giants and was especially close to manager Leo Durocher, a firebrand bench boss if ever there was one.

When in a pinch, Durocher knew that he could count on Kremenko, and vice versa.

This point was proven beyond a shadow of a doubt during the 1951 pennant race between the Giants and Brooklyn Dodgers.

During the second inning of a critical game at the Polo Grounds, Leo was coaching at third base when his slugging center fielder, Willie Mays, attempted to stretch a double into a triple.

Although Mays was under the tag and appeared to be safe, the umpire loudly called him "out!"

Furious with the call, Durocher argued with the arbiter and then made the mistake of kicking dirt on the umpire's trousers.

The ump wasted no time tossing Durocher out of the game, which caused a minor crisis with Giants strategy.

Since the Lip masterminded most of the Giants' moves, he decided on a plan whereby he could continue coaching–from the press box.

Cornering Kremenko, Durocher whispered that he'd stand behind Barney for the rest of the game. From time to time, Leo advised, he'd give his favorite writer a signal to flash down to his replacement third base coach.

Tickled to be a temporary part of the Giants' general staff, Kremenko agreed to the plan, and for several innings it worked to perfection.

Then in the eighth inning, the scheme went up in smoke.

The problem started when catcher Wes Westrum singled to center with what would have been the tying run.

Notoriously slow-footed, Westrum never was a threat to steal a base nor was he expected to do so on this fine day.

But strange things were happening, starting with Kremenko as quasi-coach.

After Westrum delivered this single, Barney began writing his "running" account of the game for the *Journal–American*'s late edition.

Perspiring in the August heat, in an ancient press box with no air-conditioning, the avid writer stopped typing for a moment.

Then a pause, and with his right hand, Kremenko wiped the sweat off his brow.

Just two seconds later, Westrum suddenly broke for second base in what appeared to be a brazen attempt to catch the Dodgers off guard.

But that did not happen and catcher Roy Campanella flied a perfect strike to second baseman Jackie Robinson, who had Westrum out by a country mile.

The astonished spectators, wondering why Westrum dared to steal, couldn't have known what had transpired, but Durocher did.

Slapping Kremenko gently on the back at the writer's desk, Leo blurted, "WHEN YOU WIPED THE SWEAT OFF YOUR BROW, YOU FOOL, YOU GAVE THE HIT AND RUN SIGN!"

41 | INCREDIBLE FEATS BY BASEBALL PLAYERS IN WORLD WAR II

One of the best players of all before the war was Cecil Travis of the Washington Senators. A combatant during the hellish Battle of the Bulge (Belgium, 1944–45), Travis came out of the assault with badly frozen feet. When he returned to the Senators at the conclusion of the war, he was unable to regain his prewar abilities.

Another former Senators player, Elmer Gedeon, died in action, as did Harry O'Neill, who played but one game for the Philadelphia Athletics. Ironically, Billy Southworth Jr., son of the St. Louis Cardinals manager, survived twenty-five bombing missions over Europe, but died trying to make an emergency landing at LaGuardia Field in Queens, New York, in February 1945.

Among other prospects who suffered as a result of the war was Johnny Grodzicki of the St. Louis Cardinals, who was considered a potential twenty-game winner. Because of a wound, Grodzicki was unable to use his right leg effectively and was only a shade of his former prewar self. Likewise, Cardinal infielder Frank "Creepy" Crespi lost his chance at a postwar career because of a pair of weird mishaps. First, Crespi broke his leg during an army baseball game. Then, while recovering, he participated in a wheelchair race at his hospital and rebroke the leg.

Few suffered as terribly as Philadelphia Athletics' pitcher Lou Brissie, a soldier in the Italian campaign. Wounded by shell fragments, Brissie was hospitalized with two broken feet, a crushed left ankle, and a broken left leg, as well as injuries to his hands and shoulders. Brissie not only recovered from his wounds but even joined the Athletics after the war, and developed into a first-rate pitcher.

Still another hero was pitcher Phil Marchildon of the Athletics, an airman whose plane was shot down by the Nazis. Taken to a prisoner-of-war camp, Marchildon lost thirty pounds over a period of a year, but survived. When he returned to the United States, his physical condition was so precarious that many doubted he would pitch again. However, the Athletics' manager Connie Mack persuaded Marchildon into putting on a uniform for Phil Marchildon Night. More than thirty thousand Philadelphians turned out to cheer Phil, who responded by pitching three innings. A year later, he was pitching like the Marchildon of old, winning thirteen and losing sixteen for the Athletics. His best season was 1947, when he went 19–9.

42 | FROM HOCKEY GOALIE TO BASEBALL MANAGER

When semipro baseball was a big deal throughout Western Canada in the 1940s, Emile Francis managed some of the best Canadian teams. But during the winter, Francis' night job was as a goaltender.

Francis, who played goalie for the Chicago Blackhawks and New York Rangers, also was an accomplished shortstop.

One of his more power-packed teams was the North Battleford (Saskatchewan) Beavers from Francis' hometown. It was a club loaded with black players, many of whom made their way to the American and National Leagues.

"We played in the old Western Canada League," Francis recalls. "Later its name was changed to the Canadian-American League. In any case, we had some of the best players on the continent. One year, no less than twenty-six were signed out of our league in to the majors."

Such accomplished Major Leaguers as Don Buford, Ron Fairly, and Tom Haller played for and against Francis, not to mention a number of superb college stars. "They couldn't play professional ball in the States," Francis remembers, "so they'd come up to Canada, get paid, and get good experience. Nobody snitched on them either."

A spunky hockey player, Francis was no less pugnacious on the diamond. He was involved in a number of bristling episodes, including one game that erupted into a full-scale riot. It took place in Rosetown, Saskatchewan, during a tournament involving teams from the United States and Cuba.

"We were playing this team—the Indian Head Cubans—and the stakes were high," says Francis. "It was something like $2,000 per man and nobody wanted to lose.

"Well on this one play, one of our players slid hard into second and upset the Cuban shortstop. Next thing we know, the whole bunch of the Cubans ran off the field and I was damned if I could figure out what they were up to; but it didn't take long for me to understand. They had gone to the bat rack and they were coming back at us with bats.

"The battle that followed took an hour and a half to cool down, but that wasn't the half of it. Two of the Cubans took off after one of our players. I could see them chase him out to the parking lot, and I followed as they went down a dirt road, heading for a farmer's house. My player was still in the lead and he made it to this farmhouse. He ran in, grabbed a butcher knife from the kitchen, and came right out at the Cubans. They were all about to go at it…when just in time the Royal Canadian Mounted Police arrived and broke it up."

By the time the dust had cleared, the game resumed and Francis' team won. He got his knife-welding player out of jail and headed for Moose Jaw for another game.

This time, the knife-wielder came up with a perfect night, five hits in five times at bat.

"After the game," says Francis, "I got a wire from the local sports editor. He wrote: 'OUT OF THE FIVE HITS YOUR MAN GOT, HOW MANY CUBANS WERE SENT TO THE HOSPITAL?'"

Francis also teamed up on the baseball field with Hockey Hall of Famers Max and Doug Bentley of Delisle, Saskatchewan, as well as other Bentley brothers. "At one time I was surrounded by Bentleys. There were five altogether on my teams. One day, a fan shouted at me: 'Francis, there's only one way you could've made this team; you must have married a Bentley.'"

43 | THE DAZZY WHO GOT THEM DIZZY

Among the long list of pitchers who combined skill with humor, Dizzy Dean ranks among the very best. Dizzy was so adept at what he did, that his accomplishments often obscured those of another mound stalwart whose named sounds a lot like Dizzy's.

That would be none other than Dazzy Vance, who—in one compelling way—could top Dean when it comes to an incredible feat.

As it happened, Dazzy didn't get Major League batters dizzy until he reached the ripe, old baseball age of thirty-one.

Vance had problems with his right arm from the inception of his career. He was never really sure what was wrong with it, either. Dazzy was sent to the minors for the 1916 season. For the next five years, his pitching record suffered because of that sore arm. Sometimes his arm hurt so badly that he didn't want to pitch, and he hardly could. He had no alternatives to playing baseball; it was the only thing he knew how to do, and he had to support his family somehow.

For a time, he soaked his arm in ice water. After a while, though, even that remedy didn't work. A doctor told Vance that if he laid off pitching for four or five years, it would probably stop bothering him. Dazzy's response to the doctor was "and how am I going to eat in the meantime?"

Vance was supposed to play for the Toledo, Ohio, team in the 1917 season. During spring training, he looked terrific. As soon as the season started, he tired easily and was soon being whipped by the opposition. Vance moved to Memphis, but the same fate awaited him there. At first, he'd shut out the batters with his fastball, and then he'd get worn out and have to leave the game. He pitched two games for the Yanks in 1918 and then returned to the minors. Spencer Abbott, manager of the Memphis team, traded Vance to New Orleans. He had no time or patience for someone who couldn't perform.

After about two weeks in New Orleans, Vance's arm began to feel better, and his pitching picked up. The following season with New Orleans, he won twenty-one games. By chance, his performance attracted the attention of the Brooklyn Dodgers.

Hank DeBerry was a New Orleans catcher who was being noticed by the Major Leagues. Larry Sutton, the Dodgers' top scout, was sent out to look at DeBerry, since the Dodgers needed a catcher badly. Sutton returned to Wilbert Robinson, manager of the Brooklyn team, to report that they should take both DeBerry and Vance.

Vance was not yet thirty-one years old, had played with a dozen different teams, and was well known for his sore arm. Nevertheless, Dazzy became a Dodger. One night in a spring exhibition game against the St. Louis Browns, Vance was pitching and faced George Sisler, one of the greatest hitters of all-time. Vance threw the first pitch, a strike. The second pitch was a strike too. With two strikes on Sisler, Vance wound up and sent a curve ball flying toward the plate. Sisler knew he was out.

Robinson was ecstatic. He hadn't known what a good buy he had found. "Anyone who can catch Sisler looking at a curve must be throwing a pretty good one," commented the Dodger manager.

From that point on, Vance was a first-rate player. In his first full season, he won eighteen games and led the league in strikeouts. His second season was a duplicate of the first. His third season was better–twenty-eight wins and only six losses. He was voted MVP.

No other pitcher has done what Vance did–he led the league in strikeouts for seven years in a row! Upon his retirement, Dazzy had won 197 games and struck out 2,045 batters. Vance was forty-five before he gave up the game. In 1954, he was voted into the Hall of Fame.

44 | THE REDHEAD WHO TURNED BASEBALL BROADCASTING INTO AN ART FORM

One of the neatest aspects of baseball as an entertainment vehicle has been the fact that the sport, over the decades, has been graced by Grade A announcers–both on radio and television.

The likes of Vin Scully, Mel Allen, Bill Mazer, and Ernie Harwell are just a few who became favorites because of their professionalism and unique style.

But the pioneer of them all was a Southerner who came to fame originally in the 1930s, handling the microphone for the Cincinnati Reds.

Red Barber not only was the voice of the Reds, but also the Brooklyn Dodgers and New York Yankees.

Barber, a Floridian by birth, emerged as the dean of baseball broadcasters on the basis of his pioneering work in the field, as well as the quality of his broadcasts, timbre of his voice, and basic objectivity; not to mention his penchant for innovation.

After working for a Cincinnati radio station, Barber became baseball's first play-by-play broadcaster. When Larry MacPhail, the Reds' general manager who fathered the idea of broadcasting the ball games, moved to Brooklyn where he ran the Dodgers, he took Barber with him.

As the "Verse of the Dodgers," Barber became a legend in his time, and so did his original phrases. Red's broadcast booth became known as the "catbird seat." When the Dodgers filled the bases, Red described the situation as "F.O.B." (full of Brooklyns). A spectacular play elicited a gushing "Oh! Doctor!" And when manager Leo "The Lip" Durocher became embroiled with umpire George Magurkirth, "the Ole Redhead" described the fracas as "a rhubarb." (Hollywood, seizing on Barber's line, later filmed a Brooklyn baseball movie called *Rhubarb*, about a cat who wanted to play for the Dodgers.)

Barber, who was behind the microphone for the 1949 Dodgers-Yankees World Series, was the first to handle the baseball telecast and also introduced the "pregame show" to the air. Red went into the Dodgers' dugout with a microphone before the season opener between the Dodgers and Giants. For the first time, thanks to Barber, listeners actually could hear the ballplayers' own voices.

Before the era when broadcasters traveled with the teams, Barber would recreate the Dodgers' "away" games from telegraph reports, which continuously poured into the studio over a Teletype machine. Occasionally, the wire would "go out," but Barber never would resort to tactics employed by other broadcasters who would simply waste time by faking action ("Jones has fouled off thirty-seven pitches in a row"). Barber explained: "I assumed my listeners knew that it was a wire recreation. I even used to have the telegraph machine close at hand, so it could be heard over the microphone. When the wire 'went out' I used to tell my listeners, 'I'm sorry, but the wire has gone out east of Pittsburgh.'"

Barber's influence was felt by all of those with whom he worked. One of the most accomplished—but unheralded—broadcasters was Connie Desmond, who groomed Vin Scully. Scully has since been the voice of the Dodgers in Los Angeles and one of the best contemporary broadcasters.

45 | A BASEBALL PUBLISHER WHO AFFECTED MORE FANS AND SERVICEMEN THAN ANYONE IN THE LITERARY BUSINESS

For more than a century, the weekly publication called *The Sporting News* was regarded as the bible of baseball.

Its publisher, J. G. Taylor Spink, often seemed more powerful than the commissioner himself, Judge Kenesaw Mountain Landis. If there were such a thing as a king of baseball journalism, Spink was that man.

To those who knew him well, Spink was both amusing and terrifying. He had a habit of waking his correspondents—working newspapermen in the big cities—at all hours of the night. Some loathed him for that, but others loved him. President Franklin Delano Roosevelt wrote Spink a fan letter during World War II. The high commands of the army, navy, and air force saluted him for getting four hundred thousand copies of *The Sporting News* to servicemen every week during the war. At a testimonial dinner for Spink in 1960, the Athletic Goods Manufacturers Association honored Spink with a Revere bowl as "America's Foremost Sports Publisher."

Colleagues remember Spink for his eccentricities. He was obsessive about punctuality and hard work. Once, a member of the staff was two hours late at the office, whereupon Spink demanded an explanation. "I was kept awake all night by a toothache," said the writer, holding his jaw. To which Spink snapped: "If you couldn't sleep, there was no reason for you to be late this morning."

According to Gerald Holland of *Sports Illustrated*, Spink probably fired most of the correspondents who worked for him. In most cases, however, the staff members returned. "When Spink's temper cooled," said Holland, "Spink usually told them a humorous story, by way of indirect apology, and frequently gave them a raise or a gift to assure them that all was forgiven."

When Spink died in 1962, one of the first to arrive at the publisher's funeral was Dan Daniel, the New York correspondent for *The Sporting News*. When someone asked Daniel why he had arrived so early, the reporter replied: "If I hadn't, Spink would have fired me for the forty-first time."

Before the invention of radar, Spink had a knack for detecting his distant correspondents and cartoonists (such as award-winning Willard Mullin of the *New York World-Telegram*) wherever they might be hiding. "Spink," said Mullin, "could get you on the pipe *from* any place, *to* any place, at *any* time."

Once, Mullin was invited by a friend to play golf on a course that he had never seen before. "All was well," Mullin recalled, "until, as we were putting on the sixth green, a messenger came galloping from the clubhouse, tongue hanging out, with the message from Garcia [Spink]. I don't know how the hell he found me, but it was him!"

On another occasion, Spink pulled the telephone off his office wall during negotiations to move the Braves from Boston to Milwaukee. The publisher had been calling Lou Perini, one of the principals in the deal, night and day in an attempt to get the scoop. He eventually got the scoop, at the expense of his phone and the wall. After several dozen calls, he phoned Perini one morning and said: "Hello, Lou. This is Taylor."

Then, responding to the inquiry from Perini, said, "Whaddya mean, Taylor who? TAYLOR SPINK."

Then, another pause to consider the question from the other end. "SPINK–S-P-I-N-K, you sonofabitch."

At which point, the phone was ripped off the wall.

Carl Benkert, a former executive for the baseball bat company Hillerich and Bradsby, attended the Kentucky Derby with Spink. "Throughout the preliminary races," said Benkert, "Spink checked the racing form and yelled at people countless times, asking opinions about which horse would win. He even went to the window to buy his own tickets."

Finally, the race began and several companions wondered which horse the publisher eventually selected. When Middleground crossed the finish line first, Spink leaped for joy. "I had him! I had $100 on his nose!"

The publisher's companions were suitably impressed until Spink's wife, Blanche, turned to her husband and then her friend. "I have news for you. He also had $100 on each of the other thirteen horses in the race!"

Spink either didn't remember or didn't see every one of his correspondents. During a trip to New York in the 1940s, he was heading for Ebbets Field in Brooklyn where he noticed that the taxi driver's license read "Thomas Holmes." Spink was curious. "Are you Tommy Holmes, the baseball writer? The one who works for the *Brooklyn Eagle?*"

The cabby's voice turned somewhat surly. "I am not," he replied to Spink. "But some crazy sonofabitch out in St. Louis thinks I am, and keeps telephoning at three o'clock in the morning!"

Red Barber, the beloved radio announcer, found a soft spot in the publisher's heart when he visited Spink's office and noticed an out-of-print book on the shelf. Spink gave it to Barber, and the broadcaster immediately offered to pay for the prize antique. Spink refused. "What could I do for you?" asked Barber.

A smile crossed Spink's face. "Be my friend," he said.

46 | THE MOST INCREDIBLE BASEBALL NICKNAME COLLECTION

O   f all the major sports, baseball takes the lead when it comes to nicknames—otherwise known as monikers or handles.

From the most famous, such as Babe Ruth, the "Sultan of Swat," to the least known, such as Emil Bildilli, whose nickname was Hillbilly Bildilli.

In between Ruth and Bildilli there have been literally thousands of nicknames-monikers-handles.

However, only three gentlemen—Chuck Wielgus, Alexander Wolff, and Steve Rushin—have actually cataloged these mostly amusing, unreal names.

Wielgus, Wolff, and Rushin actually put their collection between the covers of a book, and for a total of 192 pages have everything from Marty (Octopus) Marion to Bill (Doggie) Dawly.

Their nickname encyclopedia is called *From A-Train to Yogi: The Fan's Book of Sports Nicknames.*

Although other sports are mentioned, baseball is dominant.

Here's one of my favorites—with the authors' explanation.

John (The Count) Montefusco—Because of his name's resemblance to the title of Alexandre Dumas's novel, *The Count of Monte Cristo*. Edmonton Dantes, the fictional Count, pitched battles, while Montefusco pitched batting practice, but the difference didn't seem to matter until Montefusco moved to New York, where the media had other nickname notions. Inasmuch as the Yankees had acquired him to solve their right-handed pitching woes, Montefusco was heralded as the "Great Right Hope."

III
Unlikely Heroes

47 | ONE HAND, NO HITS—HOW CAN THAT HAPPEN?

Pitching in the Major Leagues is tough. Pitching a no-hitter is even tougher. Pitching a no-hitter, having only one hand——now that is undoubtedly the toughest task.

Left-hander Jim Abbott was born without a right hand: only a stump above the wrist at the end of his right arm. Abbott embraced the card he was dealt, though. While he could've given into his limitations, he refused to bask in self-pity and instead chose to take a different route.

"I didn't want to be defined by a disability," Abbott once said.

His drive to compete and his love for sports made up for the physical parts he lacked. At a young age, one of the sports that attracted him the most was baseball. The only question became: how could he pitch, let alone play, with only one hand?

Abbott found the answer.

"I learned to play baseball like most kids, playing catch with my dad in the front yard. The only difference was that we had to come up with a method to throw and catch with the same hand. What we came up with is basically what I continued to do my whole life."

Abbott practiced by throwing a ball against a brick wall, switching his glove off and on. When the ball bounced back to him, he flipped the glove to his left hand, ready to field.

He introduced that method in Little League, when at eleven years old, he pitched a no-hitter in his first game. He stuck with it through high school, finding further success as both a pitcher and hitter. As the University of Michigan, Abbott became one of the most talked-about baseball players in the country, winning the Sullivan Award one year, honoring the country's most outstanding amateur athlete. His nearly flawless winning percentage during college (he won twenty-six of thirty-four games he pitched for Michigan) earned him a spot on Team USA in the 1987 Pan American Games and in the 1988 Olympics.

The best, of course, was yet to come.

Abbott made it to the Major Leagues in 1989, remarkably enough, without pitching a single game in the minors. He had defied all odds and broke into the highest professional level, despite what he lacked. In his rookie season with the California Angels, he finished fifth in the American League Rookie of the Year voting. In 1991, he won eighteen games for the Angels and finished third in voting for the Cy Young Award.

To make his storybook journal even more miraculous, Abbott achieved the highlight of his career in Yankee pinstripes at perhaps baseball's most holy of grounds, Yankee Stadium.

Abbott's first season with the New York Yankees came in 1993. By September 4, 1993, he boasted only a less-than-stellar record of nine wins and eleven losses. He took the mound that day against the Cleveland Indians. Even when the game entered the eighth inning and Abbott had yet to allow a hit, the prospects of a no-hitter may have been doubtful to some. Besides, Abbott flirted with a no-hitter into the eighth that same year back in May, before losing it.

But, the eighth came and went. Eight innings passed without an Indians hit.

The Yankees held a comfortable 4–0 lead into the ninth inning, so the win was the furthest thing from fans' minds. They were anxiously hoping for the first Yankee Stadium no-hitter in ten years, and they got their wish. Abbott retired the Indians in the ninth, completing a no-hitter and adding to his laundry list of accomplishments.

Jim Abbott did not have an exceptional Major League career, but he did have his share of exceptional moments. From practicing his unorthodox pitching method against a brick wall to his no-hitter, Abbott found success at each level along the way. His perseverance, combined with his dedication and willpower, has made Abbott one of the most inspirational figures in sports.

48 | SOMEBODY ACTUALLY OUT-BABED THE GREAT RUTH [ROGER MARIS, 1961]

I n 1961, Roger Maris assaulted the record books and took on two legends: one living, one dead; one his teammate, the other the greatest player ever to take the field for the greatest franchise in the history sports. The two men I am of course referring to are Babe Ruth and Mickey Mantle.

Maris' sixty-one homers in 1961 set the single-season record, breaking Ruth's old mark of sixty, and in doing so, he outpaced Mantle—a legend in his own right—in the great home run chase of 1961, and overcame a deck that was very much stacked against him.

Maris was no Mantle or Ruth—neither in stature in the game of baseball, nor personality. He was the crew cut from Fargo, ND—a man often described as surly, quiet, or aloof—the anti-Ruth, and the opposite of the charming Mantle. Hall of Famer Rogers Hornsby summed up the general sentiment in baseball toward Maris best when he said, "Maris has no right to break Ruth's record."

Adding to storm surrounding Maris was that 1961 was no normal season for Major League Baseball to begin with. The league expanded from eight teams to ten and lengthened the season from 154 games to the familiar 162, raising questions as to what would happen if any records were broken—would it count? Should there be separate records?

As the M&M boys neared Ruth and the affront to his record became serious, Commissioner Ford Frick spoke out on the matter and declared that any record set in more than 154 games would be a separate record—not the official mark. In other words, for Maris to be the "real" home run king, he would need to hit the record-breaking dinger by game 154.

Frick, who perhaps would best be described by replacing the first consonant in his name with the letter P, was a friend of Ruth's and would've likely agreed with the aforementioned Hornsby's remark.

Hitting sixty-one home runs is no small feat, even under normal circumstances—only eight times has that magical mark been met or equaled. The point is that hitting sixty home runs is phenomenally difficult, but to do it with the literal weight of the world on your shoulders and most of baseball rooting for you to fail? Seemingly impossible—and it's this fact that makes Maris' 1961 so remarkable.

Maris dealt with booing (even in his own ballpark), viscous hate mail, and sports writers who were intent on tearing him down. In fact, the pressure got to be so much, that Maris' hair began to fall out from stress. Perhaps no fact describes just how lowly regarded he was, even by his own fans, than this sad but true anecdote:

When Maris finally did hit the record breaker in the final game of the season, he did so in a half-empty Yankee Stadium. The plaque in Yankee Stadium's monument park saluting Roger Maris' 1961 season reads "against all odds," and it's difficult to describe it any better than that—because in 1961, for all that Maris *wasn't* (wasn't good enough, wasn't worthy, wasn't a true Yankee), he *was* the man who broke the unbreakable record.

49 | THE FORGOTTEN PITCHER WHO BEFUDDLED THE BABE

While it's generally acknowledged that Babe Ruth was *the* most intimidating batter for any pitcher to confront, there was one hurler who turned the intimidation factor on the Babe.

His name was Hubert Shelby "Hub" Pruett. He pitched for the St. Louis Browns and drove the Yankees slugger nuts with his assortment of pitches.

Judging by Ruth's impotence at bat against Pruett, the Babe could have been mistaken for a fourth-string pinch hitter instead of "the Sultan of Swat." By contrast, Pruett was more like Grover Cleveland Alexander. The first time "Hub," as a Browns rookie, pitched against the Babe, he struck him out. Any suggestions that the feat was a fluke were soon dispelled. Ruth struck out nineteen out of the next twenty-three times he batted against Pruett.

50 | THE MOST INCREDIBLE HITTER OF FOUL BALLS

There are many ways to antagonize a pitcher both verbally and with a bat. Many hurlers will confess that a foul ball belter can drive them loony while wearing a pitcher down at the same time.

Such a master at fouling off pitches was Luke Appling, a Hall of Famer who starred for the Chicago White Sox. Appling enjoyed a lifetime .310 batting average with Chicago in the 1940s, but the record books fail to indicate Appling's unerring proclivity for whacking foul balls, deliberately as well as accidentally.

Once, Appling unleashed a rash of fouls in protest against the New York Yankees' management, which had failed to provide a few passes for Luke's friends when the White Sox visited the Bronx. During batting practice that day, witnesses reported that Appling hit a gross of foul balls into the stands. Since the Yankees paid for the balls, the bill was infinitely higher than it would have been for the free tickets.

Appling occasionally used the foul ball for strategic purposes. Once, when he was facing Yankees pitcher Red Ruffing, Appling took two quick strikes and appeared headed for a quick exit from home plate. Luke was disturbed since the White Sox had two men on base and there were two out.

It was time to slow down Ruffing, so Appling fouled off the next four pitches until Ruffing threw one so wide that Luke didn't bother reaching for it. He then fouled six consecutive pitches until Ruffing hurled two more egregiously bad pitches, which Luke ignored. The count now was three and two, as Ruffing bore down once more; but so did the king of the fouls. For his *chef d'oeuvre*, Appling fouled the next fourteen pitches in a row before Ruffing, frazzled and furious, finally walked Appling to fill the bases.

Impatient, Ruffing grooved a magnificent strike down the middle, which the next batter, Mike Kreevich, lined for a double. That catapulted Yankee Joe McCarthy out of the dugout to remove his ace. On his way to the showers, Ruffing paused for a few words with Appling at third base: "You did it! You did it with those bleepin' foul balls!"

51 | A ONE-ARMED OUTFIELDER IN THE MAJORS? INCREDIBLE, BUT TRUE

This could only happen during the World War II years, when many former Major Leaguers were serving in the armed forces.

Short on talent, the St. Louis Browns searched for a center fielder, and they found one in Pete Gray, whose real name was Peter Wishner. Previously, he had been a star with semipro teams in the New York area.

As a batter, Gray would take a normal swing; except that out of necessity, he held the bat in one hand. In the outfield, Gray handled fly balls by catching them in his long, thin, unpadded glove. Then, in an intricate maneuver, he would slip the glove under his armpit, roll the ball across his chest to his throwing arm, and peg the ball to the infield. On grounders to the outfield, Gray would trap the ball with his glove, then push the ball in front of him, slip off the mitt, and toss the ball back to the infield.

Despite the novelty of a one-armed player, Gray's appearance in the Browns' lineup was no gimmick. He hit .218 and was an adequate fielder. After the 1945 season, Gray returned to the minors.

There are those who argue that the Browns never should have replaced the 1944 pennant-winning center fielder, Mike Kreevich, with Gray. Kreevich was a better fielder and hitter. Gray was more of a curiosity.

The Browns also were responsible for another unusual player, Eddie Gaedel, a little person with dwarfism, who was hired by club president, Bill Veeck. Gaedel had one at-bat, on August 19, 1951, in the second game of a doubleheader, was walked, and never played again.

52 | IT TOOK A PAIR OF PITCHERS TO STOP JOE DIMAGGIO'S CONSECUTIVE GAME STREAK AT FIFTY-SIX

For a time, it appeared that DiMaggio would never stop getting at least one hit for the New York Yankees during the 1941 baseball season.

The same feeling was shared after he had stretched the streak to fifty-six games.

But that's where Al Smith and Jim Bagby came in for the Cleveland Indians.

The Tribe faced the Yankees in a night game on July 17, 1941, before 67,468 fans at Cleveland. A day earlier, DiMaggio, alias "the Yankee Clipper," had produced three hits to extend his streak to fifty-six games. To thwart Joe the next day, the Indians came up with left-handed Smith, one of the better pitchers in the American League.

It looked like DiMaggio would come through on his first at bat; he whacked a hot ground ball along the third base line, but the Indians' Ken Keltner stabbed the ball and pegged out DiMaggio. The second time up, Joe D. was walked. For his third trip, DiMaggio duplicated his first blow and, again, Keltner was the culprit, nabbing the ball and tossing Joe out at first.

But DiMaggio would get one more opportunity, in the eighth inning with a runner on first. Cleveland's player-manager Lou

Boudreau, who played shortstop, had brought in Jim Bigby, a right-handed knuckleballer, as a relief pitcher, and DiMaggio responded with an erratically bouncing grounder to deep short. Boudreau got to the ball and converted it into a double play, and the Clipper's streak had ended. DiMaggio had managed a hit in every game for more than two months, breaking the old record by fifteen.

IN 1959, WHY DID LOS ANGELES BASEBALL FANS HONOR A MAN THEY HAD NEVER SEEN PLAY FOR OR AGAINST THEIR CALIFORNIA TEAM?

Roy Campanella, a Hall of Famer and one of the greatest catchers of all-time, played for the Brooklyn Dodgers from 1948 to 1957. Prior to playing in Brooklyn, he played in the Negro Leagues and was one of the pioneers in breaking the color barrier.

In January 1958, while still a member of the Dodgers, Campy was tragically paralyzed from the shoulders down in an automobile accident. Throughout 1958, the Dodger's first year in Los Angeles, Campanella was secluded in his hospital room, visible only to his wife and doctors.

In 1959, following extensive rehabilitation, he was released from the hospital, although permanently confined to a wheelchair.

On May 7, 1959, the New York Yankees and the Los Angeles Dodgers played an exhibition game in his honor. Before the game started, friend and shortstop, Pee Wee Reese, wheeled him in to the Los Angeles Coliseum.

He then made a speech from second base to the 93,103 fans in attendance, at the time a record for the largest crowd to attend a

Major League game. The proceeds from the game went to defray Campanella's medical bills.

Between the fifth and sixth innings, the coliseum lights were cut, and announcer John Ramsey asked fans to rise, holding a lighted match or cigarette lighter in tribute to Roy.

Vince Scully, the Dodgers' announcer, called the demonstration "Ninety-three thousand prayers for a great man."

54 | THE OTHER OLE RELIABLE

Thanks to his clutch hitting, New York Yankees slugger Tommy Henrich earned the nickname "Ole Reliable."

But when it came to the Bombers' pitching staff, the same moniker would fit Allie Reynolds.

Through the history of Yankees championship seasons, there was no Bronx hurler who could top Reynolds when it came to winning the big game.

When it comes to identifying a particular season for Reynolds—alias "the Chief"—evidence of his timely excellence in the 1951 campaign stands above all.

Had it not been for the Chief's huge wins, the Yankees never would have won the American League pennant en route to the World Series.

A double-dip of no-hitters were Allie's headline grabbers. The first no-hitter took place in midsummer while, the second—an even more important one, which had happened in early fall—came during a tirade homestretch drive.

By July 12, 1951, the Yankees were in desperate need of a victory. They had lost three in a row in Boston, and two of three in Washington; they had dropped to third place.

The sizzling Cleveland Indians were coming to town with Bob Feller on the mound. Casey Stengel chose Reynolds to start for the Yankees. Gene Woodling blasted a home run over the right field fence for the first and only run of the game.

The Yankees got the win they needed, and Reynolds pitched the first of his two no-hitters.

As for the Fabulous Finale, it came on September 28, 1951. The Red Sox were the opponent at Yankee Stadium. Allie was killing them all game long. Nobody reached second base; nobody would have reached any base at all if it weren't for a few walks.

The Yankees gave Reynolds all the support he needed. They scored two runs in the first and added two more in the third. Gene Woodling hit a home run, which eventually made it 8–0.

Reynolds took his position on the mound to start the ninth inning, and the 39,038 spectators were waiting in anticipation for the Chief to finish off his second no-hitter.

Charley Maxwell fouled out to lead off the inning. Next up, Dom DiMaggio battled Reynolds, earning himself a walk. Reynolds made quick work of Johnny Pesky by striking him out.

After the strikeout, the great Ted Williams made his way to the plate. Recognizing that he was one of the best hitters, catcher Yogi Berra trotted out to the mound to calm down Reynolds.

After a quick chat, Reynolds started Williams off with a blazing fastball for the first strike. The second pitch was fouled high in the air behind home plate. Yogi could not make the catch on the high pop-up, forcing Reynolds to throw another pitch to one of the greatest hitters of the generation.

Reynolds was filled with confidence and decided to throw Williams another fastball. Williams popped it up again between home plate and the dugout.

Yogi was able to track down this fly ball and end the game. Not only was this Reynolds' second no-hitter of the season, but the Yankees clinched a share of the pennant that day.

After another clutch performance by Reynolds, Casey Stengel walked up to the Chief in the clubhouse, shook his hand, and said, "You can have the rest of the season off."

55 | WHEN NINETEEN YEARS OF GREATNESS MAY NOT QUALIFY FOR THE HALL OF FAME

Although the New York Yankees failed to gain a playoff berth during the 2013 season, the sting was considerably softened by one of their oldest players.

From the start of training camp through the final game of the season, the then-forty-three-year-old Mariano Rivera attracted so much attention in his farewell season that it often distracted fans and critics from the Bombers' shortcomings.

The Yankees' glorious closer did a farewell tour to end all farewell tours, and when it concluded at Yankee Stadium near the campaign's end, virtually everyone agreed that the classy hurler had done right by the game.

However the question remains, "Will the game do right by Mariano?"

Specifically, a continent-wide debate began as to whether he belongs in the Baseball Hall of Fame.

Many officials at Cooperstown would welcome someone who has accomplished so many remarkable feats. Yet, there's a significant block of dissent, and those critics became very vocal.

Their argument was that a pitcher who essentially pitched one inning out of nine hardly merits entrance into the diamond Pantheon. And the debate will continue until the voting takes place.

The pro-Rivera bloc has marshaled many an argument in favor, particularly given the odds he overcame between 2012 and 2013.

Rivera's career appeared to be over in May 2012.

While retreating for a fly ball in the outfield during batting practice in Kansas City, Rivera fell awkwardly on his side. The scene was hard to watch. Mariano Rivera, reaching for his right knee, grimaced in pain.

The New York Yankees' players, coaches, management, and fans hoped for the best, but Rivera's initial reaction said it all. He had torn his ACL in his right knee—a possible career-ender for any athlete. But Rivera is not just any athlete.

He proved that to be true when he returned for the start of the 2013 season—his final season. He defied the odds. At the ripe age of forty-three, Rivera came back from a horrific injury, only to show that he could still be as effective as ever. Even in his final years, Rivera was just as reliable as he was when he was saving games for the Yankees' championship teams in the late 1990s.

Playing in New York can be tough for many players, but Mariano Rivera made it look easy. For nineteen years, the man known as "Mo" thrived in an environment every Little Leaguer dreams about playing in. He dressed in those revered pinstripes and pitched in pressure situations in front of sold-out crowds, in one of the most historic ballparks to date. For nineteen years, he put on a show. His resume speaks for itself.

- Thirteen-time All-Star
- Five-time World Series Champion
- Five-time American League Rolaids Relief Man Award
- Three-time Delivery Man of the Year Award
- 1999 World Series Most Valuable Player Award

To top it off, Rivera holds the Major League Baseball record for career saves. All of these accolades can be attributed to his ability to master one pitch: the cut fastball, better known as "the cutter." Throughout his career, Rivera threw the cutter almost exclusively. Opposing teams might as well have just thrown away the scouting reports on Rivera. He was an open book. Hitters knew what was coming, yet Rivera still came out on top.

Rivera didn't just win battles against hitters; he dominated them. He could make anyone look silly at the plate, baffling both left- and right-handed batters. With lefties, Rivera attacked the inside part of the plate. With righties, he kept the ball away.

In a June *New York Times* article profiling Rivera, longtime Yankees' teammate Andy Pettite said that Rivera's dominance was due in part to his ability "to command the zone." In short, Rivera could always throw a pitch where and how he wanted. Even scarier for hitters was the fact that the cutter had late movement. Now that's pretty good.

Mo built a Hall of Fame-worthy career around throwing one pitch, in one inning at a time, with one team. The stamina and loyalty that Rivera possessed through his career is rarely found in baseball, and those traits, along with his consistency, have made him one of the game's most special treasures.

56 | THE MOST CURIOUS HOME RUN EVER BELTED

Round-trippers are usually easy to discern with the naked eye.

And if that doesn't work, video replay usually can track the home run wherever it happens to sail.

But over the years, there have been some strange four-baggers. To isolate the craziest of all, we have to zero in on the Federal League.

This outlaw circuit functioned during the early days of World War I (1914–1915). It competed with the American and National Leagues, but is carefully noted by sports historians.

As for the zany home run, it originated because of an umpire.

Barry McCormick failed to show up for the opening game of a series in Chicago between the Brooklyn Feds and Chicago Whales. McCormick's partner, Bill Brennan, worked the game alone from behind the pitcher's mound. Brennan survived without incident until the fifth inning.

At that point, a Brooklyn batter fouled off pitch after pitch, totaling twenty. Brennan trotted back and forth for more balls, and stuffed them in his shirt. It was a warm afternoon, and soon Brennan had worked up a good sweat. In disgust, he dumped a pile of balls on the ground in back of the pitcher's mound, stacked them into a neat pyramid, and mopped his brow in relief as the batter was finally retired.

Up came Grover Land, the Brooklyn catcher who had jumped to the Feds from Cleveland, where he had been a battery mate of the celebrated Addie Joss. On the first pitch, Land rifled a line drive straight into the pyramid of balls, touching off a volcanic eruption of horsehides. In the resulting scramble, each Chicago infielder came up with a ball and was waiting for the hitter as he tore around the bases.

"I was tagged five times," recalled Land, "but Brennan ruled there was no put out since it was impossible to figure out which was the fairly batted ball." Brennan decided to award Land a home run.

The Northside ballpark—now the site of Wrigley Field—resounded with anguished screams as Joe Tinker, player-manager of the Chicagos, protested the decision to James A. Gilmore, the league president. After suitable deliberation, Gilmore ruled that he would not throw out the game unless subsequent result had a deciding effect on the pennant race. It didn't, so Grover Land could always claim the world's record for freak home runs—with an assist, of course, from umpire Brennan.

57 | BILL VEECK'S STUNT TO END ALL STUNTS—SIGNING AND THEN PLAYING A MIDGET

One of the keenest promoters ever to sit behind a baseball owner's desk, Bill Veeck was notorious for his off-the-wall stunts, many of which worked to his advantage.

Never one to avoid a good punch line, Veeck once picked up the phone when a fan called to learn what time the game started, to which Veeck shot back, "What time can you get here?"

While running the Cleveland Indians in the years following World War II, Veeck—as in *wreck*—signed aging pitcher Satchel Paige when most baseball men figured that the legendary hurler was too old to help any team, let alone Cleveland. But Veeck—with a lot of help from Ole Satch—showed them.

Pitching splendidly, Paige helped the Indians win the American League pennant.

Life with the Indians was a bowl of cherries for Bill, but if there was one thing he liked almost as much as winning, it was a challenge. That helps explain why baseball author Bert Randolph Sugar once described Veeck as "baseball's premier promoter and professional gadfly."

Much to the dismay of many other Major League Baseball owners, the gadfly aspect appeared too often to suit them, especially

on the morning of July 5, 1951, when Veeck bought the belea-
guered St. Louis Browns.

To say that the Brownies had become baseball's laughingstock
would be to underplay the derision vented toward the American
League's perennial—except for 1944—losers. Just hours after
newswires proclaimed that the Browns were, in fact, purchased
by Veeck, critic John Lardner responded by writing, "Many were
surprised to know that the Browns could be bought; because they
didn't know that the Browns were owned!"

Nor did Veeck disagree. One of his first observations after
taking over the seventh-place team was simply this: "My
Browns are unable to beat their way out of a paper bag with a
crowbar."

With that in mind, Veeck realized that it would take time to
rebuild the team and, in the interim, he had to devise schemes
to regain St. Louis fans' interest. He began by signing Paige once
more, only this time as a relief pitcher. To capitalize on Satchel's
age, Veeck insisted that he occupy the bullpen *in a rocking
chair*, until called upon to pitch.

Among other moves, Veeck hired ex-Cardinal stars Marty
Marion and Harry (The Cat) Brecheen as coaches while Hall of
Fame pitcher Dizzy Dean was signed as a radio announcer.

But Veeck knew that he needed a genuine blockbuster move
and, being the genius that he was, found one in a short story by
author James Thurber. The humorist-writer told about a little
person with dwarfism (Veeck referred to as a *"midget"*) named
Duke du Monville, who came to the plate. Veeck also recalled that
New York Giants manager John McGraw once had a hunchback
mascot named Eddie Bennett. Quickly, the brainstorm jelled in
Veeck's head.

Boisterous Bill decided that he, too, would utilize a bat-
toting *midget* to score a promotion to end all Brownie promotions.

And to ensure that a big crowd—unusual for the Browns—showed up, Veeck contacted the beer company that sponsored his broadcasts and, sure enough, the Falstaff suits agreed to Veeck's promise of "something terrific" at an upcoming doubleheader. Of course none of the Falstaff executives had a clue that the Brownies' boss had a very small man in mind.

Finding the right midget was not all that difficult. Veeck contacted a Chicago actors agency, which responded by offering the club one Eddie Gaedel, elfin-sized (three feet, seven inches) compared to the average baseball player. To pull off this astonishing surprise, Bill maintained the secret of Gaedel's future appearance by not informing anyone in the media that the midget was arriving in St. Louis. Pursuing the caper to the limit, Veeck obtained a Little League-type uniform from the son of a Browns' executive with the number 1/8 on the back.

After a high-level conference, it was decided that the extravaganza would unfold in the second game of a Sunday doubleheader with the Detroit Tigers on August 19, 1951. Embellishing the event even more, Bill ordered a large birthday cake, a pair of elf's shoes, and a new set of game programs with the number 1/8 imprinted in the Brownies roster. Meanwhile, more than eighteen thousand fans awaited the big moment. It was the largest crowd to attend a Browns game at Sportsman's Park in many seasons.

Building up to the climactic event, St. Louis lost the opening game to Detroit, and then the surprising production was set in motion. Vintage automobiles and some couples in Gay Nineties costumes opened the festivities. Then, Satchel Paige and some wandering troubadours serenaded the audience. Meanwhile, the Falstaff executives remained puzzled by the "something special" that Veeck had promised, but they didn't have to wait very long.

At last, a seven-foot cake was wheeled on to the field, leaving just about everyone wondering what that was all about. Veeck answered that by cutting the cake open, whereupon Gaedel emerged. To say the least, the Falstaff officials were militantly underwhelmed. One of them beefed out loud: "A goddamn *midget*," one snapped, "what's so goddamn 'special' about that?"

It required one inning for the answer. After the Tigers were retired in the top of the first, it was the Brownies' turn at bat. Before anyone from the home team walked into the batter's box, the public address announcer took hold of the microphone and intoned to the crowd: *Attention, please. Now batting for St. Louis, Number One-Eighth, Gaedel–batting for Saucier.*

While many St. Louisans got a case of lockjaw, Little Eddie strutted to the batter's box holding a five-year-old's bat. Furious, Saucier looked up at Veeck in his owner's box and shook an angry fist at him: "Veeck waved back," commented Sugar, "and so did all the Falstaff executives, now sure of what Veeck meant when he promised 'something special.'"

No less furious was home plate Umpire Ed Hurley, who immediately called time, insisting that the burlesque be ended here and now, and without further ado. Hurley summoned Browns manager Zack Taylor to the plate, pointed at Gaedel, and demanded, "Get him out of here!"

Well prepared for the umpire, Taylor pulled an official American League player's contract out of his pocket and waved it in front of Hurley's face. Faced with the legal document, the umpire concluded that the show must go on, and then he ordered Tigers pitcher Bob Cain to start hurling.

Never confronted by a *midget* batter before, Tigers catcher Bob Swift figured that the only way to handle this unique situation was to get on his knees and hope for the best. Meanwhile, Cain desperately tried to discern just where the strike zone might be. He concluded that it was about one-third the size of a normal one and pitched to that spot.

Ball One.

Cain tried again.

Ball Two.

Hmmmm. "The strike zone seemed to be getting even smaller," noted Sugar.

Ball Three.

Meanwhile, exulting in the moment, Gaedel was enjoying rare feelings of superiority; as if he might line a single to center. But before he decided to become a hitter, Eddie remembered Veeck's words of warning: "Swing at a ball and you'll be shot!"

Ball Four.

Like any Brownie, Eddie tossed away his miniature bat and trotted to first base. Once he stepped on the bag, Taylor sent one of his regulars, Jim Delsing, in to run for him. Gaedel patted him on the toosh, but instead of returning to the dugout, he addressed the crowd of 18,369 by waving his cap to them like a pre-rock 'n' roll rock star.

The majority of fans saluted Gaedel, and even such hard-boiled journalists such as Bob Broeg of the *St. Louis Post-Dispatch* allowed that the episode touched his heart. In fact, Broeg pulled Gaedel aside and whispered, "You're always what I wanted to be—an ex-big leaguer." While headlines about Gaedel made front-page news across North America, American League owners swung into action and wrote a new rule into the books; the use of midgets was *verboten.*

As Sugar explained, "The owners sought to expunge from the record books the one at-bat of the smallest man ever to play in the Majors, without even an asterisk. But it was a moment that will live in baseball forever, a giant achievement in the cloak of a promotion."

Meanwhile, while enjoying one of his singular moments of egomania, Veeck put it his way: "I want to be remembered as 'The Man Who Helped the Little Man!'"

58 | THE JEWISH SLUGGER WHO GOT A NICKNAME LIKE BABE RUTH

They called him "The Rabbi of Swat."

That was after Babe Ruth had earned the handle "the Sultan of Swat."

One problem: Moses Solomon was not quite as good as the Babe.

Back in 1923, Giants' scout Dick Kinsella brought up a boy named Moses Solomon to manager John McGraw. McGraw worried about the fame that Babe Ruth was bringing to the rival Yanks. He was afraid that one day the Giants would play second fiddle to the Yanks. Someone had to be found to attract fans to the Giants as well. McGraw knew it would be impossible to find another Ruth. The only thing he could hope for was to keep bringing in new and impressive names to the Giants. McGraw knew that Bill Terry, Frankie Frisch, Dave Bancroft, and Lindy Lindstrom would certainly draw a crowd, but enough to counteract the Babe?

Then McGraw came up with a new idea. Observing how many Jewish people in Upper Manhattan and the Bronx were loyal baseball fans, he reasoned that bringing a good Jewish player to the team might attract attention and woo the Jewish fans from the Babe and the Yanks. That's when Kinsella found Moses Solomon.

Proclaiming that "Solomon is as big as a house, can play first base like Sisler, hit like Ruth, and fight like Dempsey," Kinsella told reporters that his new friend was "the million-dollar player McGraw has been seeking." All these extravagant claims left the other Giants a little skeptical about Solomon. Nonetheless, they quickly found him a suitable nickname, "the Rabbi of Swat."

Solomon's career was, unfortunately, short-lived. He appeared in only two games. Making three hits in those two trials, it looked as though he would live up to his new nickname. McGraw realized, however, that Solomon was just too crude for Major League competition. By the end of the year, Solomon had played for Toledo, Pittsfield, Waterbury, and Bridgeport. He then disappeared from the game.

The Dodgers had the identical problem; they had to find players to compete with Ruth's fame as well. Dodger owner Charles Ebbets came up with what he thought was the answer. Wally Simpson, who "hit almost as many home runs as Solomon," was Ebbets' answer to the problem. "He's a Yonkers boy with a big local following, and you're going to be hearing plenty about him," declared the Dodgers' chieftain.

But Brooklyn heard less about Simpson than they did about Solomon. Simpson suffered an injury on ice that winter, reporting to the Dodgers with a sprained ankle. In one game against the Phillies, he stepped in as a pinch hitter, chalked up a double, and then retired from the game after his sister's funeral.

Neither Simpson nor Solomon, both seemingly promising players, were the answers to Ruth's fame.

IV
Incredible Feats

59 | A REMARKABLE PUN THAT ONLY FRENCHY COULD UTTER

Well before Yogi Berra signed on with the Yankees, the funniest player in the majors wore a Brooklyn Dodgers uniform. Stanley (Frenchy) Bordagaray was purchased by the Bums in (1942) because the Flatbush nine needed a pinch-runner and utility outfielder-infielder. During his stint in the Pacific Coast League, Frenchy—he was really Hungarian but sported a French-type pencil moustache—was notorious for his speed on the base paths.

Once with Brooklyn, Bordagaray tried to show off his Mercury-like moves whenever possible, and on this occasion he was placed on first as a pinch-runner. Sensing he had a chance to steal second, Frenchy tore up the base path and appeared to have slid safely under the tag.

There was only one problem; umpire George Magerkurth disagreed and called "Out!"

Furious with the decision, Bordagaray leaped to his feet and began assailing the umpire with invective not yet invented and in the process accidentally spat on Magerkurth's neat, clean umpire's jacket.

Noting the unwanted spittle, Magerkurth promptly gave an emphatic heave-ho to the Dodger, who had no choice but to head for the clubhouse. But that was only the beginning of Frenchy's woes. He was immediately socked with a $50 fine and suspended for two games, harsh punishment for a part-time player.

When the fine and suspension were announced the next day, several reporters confronted Bordagaray at his dressing room locker to obtain his view of the self-inflicted mess.

"So, Frenchy," one of the scribes inquired, "how do you feel about getting thrown out of the game and then being suspended for a pair, and also fined fifty bucks for accidentally spitting on Magerkurth?"

Bordagaray pondered the query for a moment and succinctly replied with incredible logic: *"That was more than I expectorated."*

Frenchy-watchers insist that *that* was the best play—on words—of Bordagaray's career.

60 | AN INCREDIBLY CORNY CONVICTION

I t's hard to believe that a baseball manager could get thrown out of a game because of popcorn, but it did happen once. In this case the culprit was an early baseball clown—but also a darn good player and later coach—named Germany Schaefer.

One day, when his team was playing a less talented club, Schaefer showed up in the coach's box with an oversized bag of popcorn and then proceeded to pay more attention to the confection than the game. Not only would Germany eat the popcorn, but sometimes he'd "feed" it to imaginary birds and squirrels, not to mention his friends in the grandstands.

Not surprisingly, Schaefer's shenanigans amused everyone but the opposition and the umpires. Enemy pitchers complained that the popcorn machinations distracted their concentration and demanded an end to on-field popcorn.

"Germany's routine ended during a game against the White Sox," wrote baseball author Dan Morgan. "While nibbling on Cracker Jacks this time, the umpire sent Schaefer to the showers."

But before heading for the clubhouse, Germany asked the umpire why he was being given the heave-ho.

"Because," the umpire concluded, "you're committing an act contrary to the best interests of the game."

On-field popcorn has never been a deterrent to pitchers since then.

61 | HOW YOGI BECAME A STAND-UP COMIC

Yogi Berra is in the Baseball Hall of Fame because of his catching prowess and ability to hit virtually any kind of pitch, anytime, anywhere. Yet, for all Berra's accomplishments behind the plate for the Yankees and as a World Series hero, the St. Louis native is notorious for his famed stand-up lines such as "It ain't over 'til it's over."

But what was the *very first* Yogi-ism that began an endless string of precious punch lines?

It all began in the catcher's rookie year when Yankees manager Bucky Harris desperately tried to halt Berra's annoying habit of swinging at bad balls.

"When you get to the plate," urged Harris, "do me a favor and *think just a little*. Think of the fact that you've got three strikes to pick from the kind of pitch you want. Think of the kind of ball you're likely to get when the pitcher is behind and when he's ahead. Just do a little thinking with your swinging, and you'll be all right."

Armed with those words of wisdom, Yogi strode to the plate and proceeded to take three straight strikes. Not once did the bat leave his shoulders.

After returning to the dugout, Berra was met by his irate manager. Naturally, Harris wanted an explanation which, of course, Yogi had.

"How come you took three strikes without so much as a half-swing?" Bucky demanded.

"Aw nuts," Berra shot back, "how kin ya think an' swing at the same time!"

And, if you're wondering how Lawrence Berra got the nickname Yogi, it dates back to his teenaged years growing up in the Hill section of St. Louis. When he was a squat fifteen-year-old, his pals thought he looked like a squatting yogi who had been featured in a recent movie. Before that, his family had nicknamed him "Lawdy." With his nickname in mind, Berra once opined, "If I walked down the street and somebody yelled, 'Hey, Larry,' I know that I wouldn't turn around."

(Postscript: Although he never went to college, for years Yogi has been the headman at a New Jersey museum, of all things. What could be more incredible than a Yogi Berra Museum that sits on the campus of Montclair State University in Little Falls, New Jersey? The museum also has a "Learning Center," and if you've heard some of his Yogi-isms, you would agree that having his own museum learning center is quite an incredible feat in and of itself.)

62 | HOW TO SQUELCH AN UMPIRE— AND GET AWAY WITH IT

Over the decades Major League umpires have been notoriously sensitive about the profession and proficiency at handling it. Those who insult the arbiters do so at their own risk and often pay a heavy price (see French Bordagaray). But one individual who miraculously escaped punishment after squelching an umpire was Nick Altrock, former pitcher, coach, and among the all-time funnymen among umpire-baiters.

He proved this point while at bat one day. Nick poled a fastball into the left field stands that just happened to bean a female spectator. While the lady was keeling over in her seat, the umpire shouted, "Foul ball!" He then turned to Altrock and blurted, "I sure hope that woman was not badly hurt 'cause she sure was knocked out cold."

After listening attentively, Nick deadpanned his reply: "Knocked out? Not at all. She just heard you call that one *right*— and fainted from shock!"

63 | THE GREATEST SEASON BY A MODERN-DAY PITCHER [PEDRO MARTINEZ]

There's an expression: "genius will out," which snuggly fits righty Pedro Martinez.

The native of the Dominican Republic experienced a season that could only be described as Special Deluxe.

The year was 2000, in the height of the steroid era when batters were hitting home runs as easily as they exhaled. Martinez finished 18–6 with a 1.74 ERA, four shutouts, 283 K's (11.8 per inning), and a miniscule .737 WHIP—in the process leading the league in the latter four categories.

But simply saying Martinez "led the league" doesn't even begin to tell half the story—he didn't just lead the league, but also he put every other pitcher in baseball to shame.

Martinez's 1.74 ERA in 2000—a phenomenal accomplishment even in a normal year—was almost a full point better than the next-best starter (Kevin Brown's 2.58 mark), more than twice as good as Roger Clemens' 3.70 (the next best in the home run-crazy American League), and a *full three points* better than the league average of 4.77.

To put that in perspective, Bob Gibson's 1.12 ERA in 1968 only led the league by just under half a point and was about two points better than the league average. Martinez's .737 WHIP didn't just lead the league, but also it's the lowest mark in the history of baseball—dead-ball era, live-ball era, steroid era—doesn't matter.

In the *entire history* of baseball, Pedro allowed just 5.3 hits per nine innings in 2000—1.5 better than the next-best pitcher. His strikeout-to-walk ratio was a joke: 8.875, which was more than 3.5 K's better than the next-best in the league, and the fourth-best ratio ever recorded by a pitcher in the live-ball era. I could go on and on, but doing so would be like beating a dead horse—Pedro Martinez was head and shoulders better than every other pitcher in baseball's millennial season.

The numbers Martinez complied in 2000 are phenomenally impressive—even record-setting in some cases—in any era, but to do it at the height of the steroid era is what truly makes it special. If 1968 was the year of the pitcher, then 2000 was the year all pitchers would like to forget. 5.14 runs were scored per game in 2000—the highest mark since 1936—and overgrown sluggers turned games into venerable home run derbies, as a historic all-time high of 1.17 home runs were launched into orbit per game. Combine that with a league slash line of .270/.345/.437, and suddenly the league ERA of 4.77—the second-worst of the live-ball era—makes sense.

If you took the mound in 2000, best bring a bib–because things were likely to get messy. In comparison, when Gibson flummoxed hitters in '68, the league hit just .237—lowest in history, scored 3.42 runs per game—lowest in the live-ball era, and the league ERA of 2.98 was far and away the lowest of the live-ball era. Pedro Martinez was pitching with grenades in 2000, but he miraculously kept hitters from pulling the pin.

64 | THE MOST SENSATIONAL GAME EVER PITCHED [SANDY KOUFAX]

I n the history of professional baseball (that's well over one hundred thousand games, but who's counting?), only twenty-three perfect games have been tossed. One is thrown roughly every 4,400 starts—give or take a couple hundred.

If you're a fan of percentages, that means every time you watch a baseball game, you have about .023 percent chance of seeing a perfecto—the expression "one-in-a-million" quite literally applies here.

While a perfect game is rare enough, on June 9, 1965, Sandy Koufax and Bob Hendley of the Cubs hooked up for a pitchers' duel, the likes of which had never been seen before, and hasn't been seen since a 1–0 victory for Koufax's Dodgers in which two men—no really, just two—reached base (Lou Johnson, on two walks), a record for futility that still stands today.

Koufax's exploits alone would be enough to qualify this game as amongst the best ever pitched. The splendid southpaw turned in the most dominating performance of a career full of them, striking out fourteen—including the final six—as he spun his first and only perfect game.

The fourteen K's was a record for a perfect game that has since been tied by Matt Cain, but unlike Koufax, Cain can't say he struck out Hall of Famer Ernie Banks three times when he took his turn at making history—or had to find a way to retire another Hall of Fame Cubbie, Ron Santo.

Koufax's perfecto is also remarkable for one other reason—a lack of a memorable defensive play. It seems like in every perfect game or no-hitter, there's at least one close call—it could be early, it could be late—but there's always at least one play where the man on the mound needs some help from his friends. Not so with Koufax. Scour as many accounts of the game as you want, but there's nary a description of a single hard-hit ball of off Koufax on that fateful day.

Despite Koufax's phenomenal exploits, it takes two to tango. For a game to truly be the greatest ever pitched, the man toeing the rubber for the opposing side needs to be up for the challenge as well—and all Bob Hendley did was turn in the performance of a lifetime. Hendley surrendered just one run—it was unearned, scored on a throwing error by his catcher—one hit, and two base runners all game long. In fact, Hendley carried a no-no of his own into the seventh, and only lost it on what is described in all accounts as a bloop double by Lou Johnson, who, remarkably, was the only player to reach base for either side that game (he did so twice).

There has never, in the history of baseball, been a double no-hitter, but in September '65, Koufax and Hendley came as close as anyone ever has and turned in a pair of performances that stand the test of time.

65 | YOU'RE NEVER TOO OLD TO BAT .388 [TED WILLIAMS, AGE 38]

Perhaps it's a measure of just how great the man was, but somehow, Ted Williams' miraculous 1957 season seems to slip through the cracks when discussing the Splendid Splitter's accomplishments. To explain how astonishing it was for Williams to hit .388 at thirty-eight, first we must examine just how rare it is to hit for such a high average to begin with.

The last man to hit .400 was, appropriately enough, none other than Williams himself in 1941. Since then, only *four times* has a player hit .380 or above: Williams' .388 in 1957, Rod Carew's .388 in 1977, George Brett's .390 in 1980, and Tony Gwynn's .394 in 1994 (a strike-shortened season). To put this in perspective, in the same time period, we've seen the sixty-home run barrier—once the benchmark of all virtually unattainable statistical goals—shattered seven times, the 100-steal mark equaled or bested on eight occasions, and 150 RBI met or surpassed twelve more times. The point is, players just do not hit .388 anymore—let alone when they're thirty-eight.

It's not a stretch to say that by the age of thirty-eight, most athletes—even the great ones—are, to put it generously, on their way out. This much is true, regardless of position or sport. Father Time is the one adversary that remains undefeated—and it's

this fact that makes Ted Williams' 1957 truly one for the books
(literally, in this case).

Let's take a look, for the sake of comparison, at what some of
baseball's other historically feared sluggers did at the same age.
Mickey Mantle—to whom Williams lost the MVP in '57—retired

at thirty-six. Oh, but the Mick's a bad example, you say, because of his chronic knee problems and myriad of off-the-field issues? Fair enough. How about the man Williams was once almost traded for, Joe DiMaggio? He, too, retired at thirty-six. What about a center fielder known much more for his durability than the prior two—Willie Mays? At thirty-eight, the Say Hey Kid was a kid no more—he hit .283 with just thirteen home runs, and only had one twenty-plus homer season left in him. How about a man known throughout his career for his remarkable consistency—Hank Aaron? Hammerin' Hank finally began to show some signs of age, hitting .265 with thirty-four home runs at thirty-eight. But, you ask, what about the greatest of them all? What about the legendary Babe Ruth? Even the Bambino was slowing down by thirty-eight, when he hit .301 with thirty-four homers—not bad, but certainly not Ruthian—and his lowest numbers in a full season in over a decade.

I could go on and on—look up almost any Hall of Famer, and take a peek at his numbers at age thirty-eight, and the story will undoubtedly remain the same—the signs of decline will be obvious, if the man was even fortunate enough to still be playing. But Williams is the exception.

Maybe the best way to describe his 1957 is "unimaginable"—it's unimaginable, and before Williams did it, impossible, that a thirty-eight-year-old man could hit .388 and turn in one of the best offensive seasons in baseball history. But with a bat in his hands, the Splendid Splitter had a habit of making the previously unfathomable look routine, and '57 was no exception.

66 | THE MOST INCREDIBLE WORLD SERIES GAME FEATURING A TRIPLE PLAY

I t happened in Cleveland during the 1920 World Series between the Indians and Brooklyn. What transpired still boggles the mind, almost a century later. This was the fifth game for the championship in which unusual events began happening in the very first inning.

Elmer Smith hit a bases-loaded home run over the right field fence; it was the first of its kind in a World Series game. The second unique episode occurred during a Brooklyn rally in the fifth inning with runners on first and second. Clarence Mitchell was the batter when Robins manager Wilbert Robinson signaled for a hit-and-run play; as soon as Mitchell swung, the runners were to take off. Mitchell did as instructed, belting a searing line drive over second base. Indians second baseman Bill Wambsganss was so far from the base that he appeared unable to make a play for the hit. "But," wrote Harry Cross in *The New York Times*, "Wambsganss leaped over toward the cushion, and with a mighty jump, speared the ball with one hand." Pete Kilduff, the runner on second, was on his way to third and Miller, the runner from first, was almost within reach of second.

The quick-thinking Wambsganss touched second base, retiring Kilduff, who had almost reached third base. Meanwhile, Miller, who was trapped between first and second, appeared mummified by the proceedings and remained transfixed in his tracks. Wambsganss trotted over and tagged Miller for the third out. Thus, the first unassisted triple play was accomplished in the World Series. "The crowd," reported Cross, "forgot it was hoarse of voice and close to nervous exhaustion, and gave Wamby just as great a reception as it had given Elmer Smith."

If that wasn't unusual enough, there was the added spectacle of Brooklyn pitcher Burleigh Grimes' humiliation. "No pitcher," wrote Cross, "has ever been kept in the box so long after he had started to slip. Uncle Robbie kept him on the mound for three and two-thirds innings, including two home runs and a triple.

"With a half a dozen able-bodied pitchers basking in the warm sun, Grimes was kept in the game until he was so badly battered that the game became a joke."

When the score was 7–0, Grimes finally was removed.

In an ironic contrast, Cleveland pitcher Jim Bagby was hailed as a hero, even though no pitcher was ever before pounded for thirteen hits in a World Series. "He pitched," wrote Cross, "what was really a bad game of ball, but when it was over he was proud of it."

67 | DICK GROAT—WILL IT BE BASKETBALL OR BASEBALL?

There's not much similarity between baseball and basketball, except for the fact that both balls involved are round.

As a result, it's rare to find athletes who are competent enough to star in both sports. There was, however, one significant exception: Dick Groat, who ultimately starred with the Pittsburgh Pirates, St. Louis Cardinals, and the Philadelphia Phillies.

At five feet, eleven inches, Groat played one season in the National Basketball Association until he was faced with the choice of either professional baseball or basketball and went for the former. Groat wound up his fifteen-year MLB career with a lifetime batting average of .286 and was one of the best fielding shortstops in the majors during the 1960s.

68 | THE ALL-TIME UTILITY PLAYER, MARTIN DIHIGO

One of the unfortunate aspects of baseball history is that African American players did not appear in the major leagues until Jackie Robinson broke the color barrier in 1947.

Had the year been, say, 1847 and black players populated the top rung of baseball, Martin Dihigo would be a household name among diamond fans in the manner of a Babe Ruth or Lou Gehrig.

Starring in the American Negro League—among other circuits—Dihigo became known as the ultimate utility player.

Not only did Martin pitch, but he also played every position in the field, including catcher.

Martin Dihigo, according to many observers who saw him play in the 1920s and 1930s for the Cuban Stars and Homestead Grays, was one of the ultimate ballplayers of all time.

In a 1935 East-West All-Star game, Dihigo started in center field and batted third for the East, and, in the late innings, was called upon to pitch in relief. Buck Leonard, himself a star with the Grays, and others call Dihigo the greatest ballplayer of all-time.

The Cubans and the Grays used him at every position, and in 1929 he batted .386 in the American Negro League.

When the Negro National League folded and blacks began to enter the major leagues, by this time Dihigo was too old to make it to the bigs, and he played out his career during the 1950s in Mexico.

69 | THE LONGEST HOME RUN OUT OF YANKEE STADIUM

When baseball historians rate the finest slugging catchers of any era, the name Josh Gibson invariably makes the list. The pity of it all is that he never played in the big leagues, since at the time it was composed of only Caucasian players.

As African American baseball stars go, Gibson ranks alongside Satchel Paige, Martin Dihigo, and another catcher who did make it into the National League, Roy Campanella.

How powerful a hitter was Gibson?

Quite simply, he did what no batter has ever accomplished at Yankee Stadium. Gibson hit this home run in a Negro National League game against the Philadelphia Stars.

Jack Marshall of the Chicago American Giants witnessed the feat: "Josh hit the ball over the triple deck next to the bullpen in left field. Over and out! I will never forget that because we were getting ready to leave because we were going to play a night game and we were standing in the aisle when that boy hit this ball!"

Baseball's bible, *The Sporting News*, credits Gibson with hitting a longer home run than Ruth ever hit in the old Yankee Stadium, a drive that hit just two feet from the top of the stadium wall, circling the bleachers in center field, about 580 feet from home plate.

It was estimated that had the blast been two feet higher it would have cleared the wall and traveled about seven hundred feet.

Walter Johnson, one of the best pitchers of all-time, watched Gibson in action and observed: "There is a catcher that any big-league club would like to buy for $200,000. His name is Gibson . . . He can do everything. He hits the ball a mile. And he catches so easy, he might as well be in a rocking chair. Throws like a rifle. Bill Dickey [the Yankee great] isn't as good a catcher. Too bad this Gibson is a colored fellow."

One legend has it that Gibson was playing at Forbes Field in Pittsburgh one day and hit such a towering drive that nobody saw it come down. After long deliberation, the umpire ruled it a home run. As the legend goes, a day later, Gibson's team was playing in Philadelphia when suddenly a ball dropped out of the sky and was caught by an alert center fielder on the opposition. Pointing to Gibson, the umpire ruled: "You're out—yesterday in Pittsburgh!"

70 | JUAN MARICHAL VS. WARREN SPAHN—DUEL OF THE TITANS

There are many facets to classic baseball games, but none can top a pitchers' battle.

Historians have a large selection from which to choose, but when it comes to hurlers' bouts, the one that featured Juan Marichal and Warren Spahn rarely can be topped.

On July 2, 1963, two future Hall of Famers locked up for what may not have been the most dominating, but is certainly the most astonishing, pitchers' duel of all time. One man, the twenty-five-year-old whirling dervish, Marichal, was at the height of his powers; the other, the forty-two-year-old Spahn, was a living legend, who, despite his age, was in the midst of winning twenty games for an unprecedented thirteenth time.

But, despite the extensive résumé of each man, no one in his/her wildest dreams could predict what would come next.

Over four hundred pitches were thrown as Juan Marichal's Giants defeated Warren Spahn's Braves 1–0 in sixteen innings, on the strength of a Willie Mays walk-off home run. The game was played in a brisk four hours and ten minutes—indicative of just how masterful each man was that day, and in about the same time as the average nine-inning Yankee-Red Sox tilt. And pitch counts?

What pitch counts? Both men went the distance, and when it was all said and done, the final lines looked like this:

Marichal: 16 IP, 8 hits, 0 runs, 4 BB, 10 K
Spahn: 15.1 IP, 9 hits, 1 run, 1 BB, 2 K

Take a good, long look at that, boys and girls, because as long as baseball is played, you'll never see another stat line like either of those. Nowadays, it would take many starters three outings to go as far as either man went in just one. Heck, it might take Phil Hughes a month.

Making this feat of human endurance all the more impressive are the formidable lineups Marichal and Spahn faced. In addition to the two starters, five men who would go on to earn busts in Cooperstown took the field that day: Willie Mays, Willie McCovey, and Orlando Cepeda of the Giants, and Hank Aaron and Eddie Mathews of the Braves.

San Francisco would lead the league in homers that year by a whopping fifty-eight over second-place Milwaukee. But, as the night progressed, the two hurlers continued to confound the legend-laden lineups opposing them: the southpaw Spahn, featuring the now-all-but-extinct screwball, and Marichal, with his dazzling array of pitches thrown from a variety of arm angles.

Neither man was in much trouble for most of the game. Marichal allowed three men in scoring position in the regulation nine innings—one of them Spahn, one of the greatest hitting pitchers of all time, who smoked a double off the wall—but stranded them all, with a little help from Willie Mays, who cut down a man at the plate in the fourth. Spahn, for his part, allowed a long drive to Willie McCovey in the bottom of the ninth that would've ended it, but it curved just foul (although McCovey, to this day, still disagrees with the umpire's ruling). Nevertheless, baseball is a game of inches, and whether it was a blown call, a gust of wind, or a goose fart that caused that ball to be called foul, it allowed an already historic duel to become legendary.

Spahn was seemingly on the ropes in the fourteenth when he loaded the bases, but the splendid lefty worked out of the

JUAN MARICHAL
THE DOMINICAN DANDY

jam. Amazingly, but for the trouble Spahn encountered in the fourteenth, neither hurler showed any signs of fatigue as night turned into morning. In fact, it was the presence of the older Spahn that motivated the much younger Marichal to keep going. Giants manager Alvin Dark kept asking Marichal if he wanted out, causing the man with the highest leg kick in baseball to famously quip: "Alvin, do you see that man pitching on the other side? He's forty-two and I'm twenty-five, and you can't take me out until that man is not pitching."

There's no indication Spahn ever would've removed himself from the game had Mays not ended it, and in a classic "boy, has the game changed" moment, the old lefty was known to—and it's unlikely this game was any exception—spend much of his time between innings smoking cigarettes in the runway behind the dugout.

To say we'll never again see a sixteen-inning, 1–0 game where both pitchers go the distance—let alone one in which one starter is over forty—is the understatement of the century. That's what makes Spahn and Marichal's accomplishment so unbelievable.

As the role of innings limits and pitch counts continues to grow exponentially within the fabric of baseball, we look back in increasing disbelief at what Spahn and Marichal did in 1963. Their famous duel ages like fine wine. Years later, even Spahn—in a clear indication that he understood the significance of that famous game—would remark to his son, Greg, that of the countless pitches he threw in his twenty-one-year career, it was the last pitch, that July morning, that he regretted the most. Recalled Greg: "That pitch probably bothered him more than any he ever threw. For years he said that if he had one pitch he'd like to take back, that was it."

71 | BOB GIBSON'S FABULOUS 1968 SEASON

ention the name Bob Gibson to almost any batter who faced the St. Louis Cardinals fireballer, and he will tell you the first word that comes to mind: intimidation.

Few hurlers could put more fear in the hearts of the most courageous batters than Gibson.

In the history of Major League Baseball, there are certain individual seasons that stand above the rest: Babe Ruth's 1921, Ted Williams' 1941, and, yes, Bob Gibson's 1968—the holy grail of all pitching seasons.

In 1968, Bob Gibson was 22–9, with a 1.12 ERA—a live-ball era record, twenty-eight complete games, thirteen shutouts—also a live-ball era record, and a miniscule .853 WHIP.

Imagine if, in addition to hitting .406 in 1941, Ted Williams also slugged sixty-one home runs—that's basically what Gibson did in '68. He was utterly dominant, to a degree no one had ever seen before, and hasn't been touched since.

Gibson's 1.12 ERA is almost a half-point better than the next-best mark recorded in the live-ball era—Greg Maddux's 1.56 in 1994. Furthermore, Maddux only made twenty-five starts that season, making it likely that number would have gone up had he pitched a full slate of games. Yet, the 1.12 doesn't even begin to tell the whole story.

Nestled inside the 304.2 innings Gibson tossed that year is perhaps the most dominant stretch a pitcher has ever had. From June 2 through July 30, Gibson threw ninety-nine innings and gave up a ludicrous *two runs*. That's a 0.27 ERA in what amounts to, in modern times, essentially half a season's worth of innings.

All things considered, perhaps the most baffling thing about Gibson's 1968 is that he somehow lost nine games. The biggest detriment to Gibson's greatness that season is that 1968 is commonly referred to as the "year of the pitcher." Pitching was so dominant that year, the mound was lowered the next season.

But punishing Gibson for being so devastating in 1968 would be like punishing Babe Ruth for not hitting sixty home runs in the dead-ball era; "Well, yeah, sixty's great, but it's not like he did it when home runs were hard to hit." Sound ridiculous? Thought so.

The fact is, Gibson was still head and shoulders the best pitcher in the league. His ERA was a half-point lower than his closest competitor, he tossed four more shutouts than anyone in the league, and his WAR was nearly a full three points higher than any other pitcher (11.2 to Luis Tiant's 8.4).

If that's not enough, Gibson turned in one of the most dominant performances in World Series history in '68. In Game One of the Fall Classic, Gibson tossed a complete game shutout, striking out seventeen baffled Detroit Tigers, while allowing just five hits and walking one.

The seventeen K's is a World Series record that still stands. There aren't many certainties in sports, but I am certain that as long as I live, I will never see a pitcher have a season like Bob Gibson did in 1968.

72 | A GOOSE EGG TRIFECTA FORGOTTEN BY MANY

You won't hear the name Christy Mathewson bruited around much anymore, simply because he was a pitcher who starred early in the twentieth century.

His exploits—many extraordinary—put baseball on the map in the early 1900s when he was the ace of the New York Giants pitching staff.

Many historians will tell you that Matty's performance in the 1905 Series between John McGraw's Giants and Connie Mack's Athletics never will be matched.

On October 9, 12, and 14, 1905, Mathewson threw three shutouts in a span of six days, in a series of only five games, a record that still stands today, over one hundred years later.

The three goose eggs enabled the New Yorkers to defeat Philadelphia four games to one. Joe McGinnity won the other game for the Giants in the same fashion as Mathewson: a shutout as well.

The World Series of 1907 was disappointing in only one respect. The heralded pitching duels between the brilliant, but erratic, Rube Waddell and Mathewson never materialized.

The great Philadelphia southpaw was injured in some horse-play on a railroad platform, while the A's were celebrating the clinching of the American League pennant in Boston. As a result, he was unable to pitch in the Series against the Giants.

73 | SHORT HITS—FOR NINE MEN IN THE FIELD, NINE SHORT TALES OF INCREDULITY

Author's Note: From 1990 through the present, there have been some extraordinary events on the field and off. Here are nine for your enjoyment:

A) RICKEY HENDERSON BREAKS LOU BROCK'S STOLEN BASE RECORD (1991)

Rickey Henderson became synonymous with the stolen base over the course of his long career. In 1982, Henderson stole over 130 bases, more than eleven entire teams' totals for the season. On May 1, 1991, the greatest base-stealer on the planet broke Lou Brock's career record when he stole third against the Yankees. Henderson passed Brock in just eleven big league seasons, while it took Brock nineteen years to master the feat.

B) JACK MORRIS THROWS TEN SHUTOUT INNINGS IN WORLD SERIES GAME SEVEN (1991)

The World Series of 1991 featured one of the greatest pitching matchups of all time. Amazingly, both teams finished in last place the year before, and never before had a team gone from last place to the World Series.

In Game Seven, Jack Morris squared off against John Smoltz, and it was Morris who came out on top, pitching ten shutout innings to lead Minnesota to the title. Not only was it the first 1–0 Game Seven finish since 1962, but also it was the first Game Seven since 1924 in which the hosts walked off with the victory in the bottom of an extra inning.

C) JOE CARTER'S WALK-OFF WORLD SERIES HOME RUN (1993)

Only two players in Major League Baseball history have hit a walk-off home run to win a World Series. Bill Mazeroski beat the Yankees with his walk-off homer for the Pirates in the 1960 World Series, and in 1993, Joe Carter's homer off Phillies closer Mitch Williams gave the Toronto Blue Jays the World Championship.

Carter's historic blast remains the only come-from-behind, walk-off World Series-winning home run.

D) CAL RIPKEN PASSES LOU GEHRIG (1995)

Nobody ever thought that Lou Gehrig's iron-man record would ever be broken. Gehrig's record of 2,130 consecu-

tive games played was thought to be one of those records deemed unbreakable, but Cal Ripken Jr. came along and did the unthinkable.

Throughout the 1995 season, the Orioles draped numbers on the B&O Warehouse in right field to record Ripken's streak. Finally, on September 6, in a game against the California Angels, Ripken passed the "Iron Horse," and now that record is pretty much unattainable.

E) BASEBALL RETURNS TO NEW YORK AFTER 9/11 (2001)

The Major League Baseball season was reaching the home-stretch when the 9/11 attacks took place, but Commissioner Bud Selig understandably shut down the game. When play resumed in New York on September 21, the Mets were home to take on the Atlanta Braves, in what was the first major sporting event in New York since the attacks.

The Mets and Braves had been longtime rivals, and despite the air that this particular game took on, it was still a tense, 1–1 affair through seven innings. That all changed when a one-out eighth-inning walk brought up Mike Piazza. Everybody knows what happened next, as the power-hitting catcher launched a 0–1 pitch deep over the center field fence to put the Mets ahead for good and launching an enormous celebration.

F) LUIS GONZALEZ DELIVERS WORLD SERIES TITLE TO THE DESERT (2001)

The 2001 World Series was one of the greatest World Series to ever be played. The most storied franchise in Major League history was trying to four-peat against a team that had been in existence for just four years.

These playoffs took on an even bigger significance for the Yankees, as they were playing for their city. With the city still recovering from the 9/11 attacks, Yankee games provided a much-needed distraction for New Yorkers.

The Bronx Bombers took a 2–0 deficit back to the Bronx, but they went on to win the next three games, with two of the wins coming in dramatic fashion against Arizona's closer Byung-Hyun Kim. The Diamondbacks bounced back to win Game Six and force a Game Seven, where the Yankees took a 2–1 lead to the eighth inning.

With Mariano Rivera coming into the game, another ring was all but a done-deal. Rivera breezed through the eighth inning by striking out the side. But then, the unimaginable happened. A lead-off Mark Grace single would set up a rally for the ages. Arizona would eventually load the bases to bring up Luis Gonzalez, their best hitter. With the Yankees' infield and outfield drawn in, Gonzalez blooped a ball over a drawn-in Derek Jeter to deliver the World Series title to Arizona.

G) DEREK JETER'S FLIP (2001)

Derek Jeter's name sits atop the Yankee "Mount Rushmore," with the likes of Ruth, Gehrig, DiMaggio, and Mantle, for a number of feats. Over the years, he has had countless clutch hits, and he was even nicknamed "Mr. November" during the 2001 postseason. During that same playoff run, Jeter made one of the most brilliant defensive plays ever, in Oakland.

With the Athletics leading the five-game divisional series two games to none, on the verge of completing a sweep, the Yankees took a 1–0 lead into the bottom of the seventh inning behind a strong performance from Mike Mussina.

With two outs and Jeremy Giambi on first base, Terrence Long hit a line drive into the right field corner. With Giambi rounding third base, right fielder Shane Spencer's throw sailed over both cut-off men, and it appeared that Giambi would score easily. But Jeter came out of nowhere and changed the momentum of the series with the famously known "Flip" play.

After the game, Jeter told the press that the team had been practicing this type of play all year as a result of a similarly botched throw in spring training. The idea of stationing the shortstop down the first base line on balls hit to deep right field came from Yankees bench coach, Don Zimmer.

H) HALL OF FAMERS BABE RUTH AND TY COBB'S SHARED IDOL

The renowned sluggers admitted that they revered shoeless Joe Jackson's swing so much that they watched him when they were win a slump. Shoeless Joe ranked third on the all-time batting average list with an average of .356.

I) ROY HALLADAY'S NLDS NO-HITTER (2010)

After never making it to the postseason as a member of the Toronto Blue Jays, Roy Halladay was ready for baseball's biggest stage. Halladay wanted to be a member of the Philadelphia Phillies so he could chase a Championship, and in his first postseason game, he threw just the second postseason no-hitter ever and first since Don Larsen's 1956 perfect game.

74 | THE CATCHER WHO COST THE PHILLIES $10,000 FOR RUNNING TOO FAST

This one *really* strains credulity, but it actually happened. It's all about a second-string catcher on the Philadelphia Phillies, who cost his club ten grand simply by not thinking.

Here's how this bizarre scenario unfolded.

On June 8, 1947, the Pirates and Phillies were tied in Philadelphia at 4–4 in the eighth inning. Then, in the top of the ninth, Pirate Ralph Kiner hit a home run.

It was nearly 7 p.m., and there was an early curfew in Philadelphia. If the game did not end by 7 p.m., the score reverted to the last complete inning. If there was a tie, the game would be replayed the next day as part of a doubleheader.

Both the Pirates and the Phillies were aware of this. The Pirates had little desire to play a doubleheader, but the Phillies wanted the extra $10,000 in admission tickets that a doubleheader would bring. In order to hasten the outcome of the game, the Pirates' Hank Greenberg allowed himself to be out.

When the Phillies came up, Manager Ben Chapman told his men to delay as much as possible. The first man popped out. The second man, Charley Gilbert, a pinch hitter, took an excessively long time to select a bat. Then he argued with umpire Babe Pinelli, intentionally fouled off some pitches, and finally struck out. One more out and the Phillies would lose both the game and the $10,000 gate money from a doubleheader.

Chapman called for second-string catcher Hugh Poland, stationed three hundred feet away in the bullpen, to hit, anticipating that Poland would take some time to come in, eating up the clock.

Much to Chapman's dismay, Poland ran in without realizing that the purpose of his appearance was to delay the game.

When Poland arrived, he saw that he had to counteract his dash. He argued briefly with Umpire Pinelli, but Pinelli hurried him back to the box.

Poland took two strikes and then hit a lazy fly ball, which Pirate Wally Westlake caught—fifty-two seconds before curfew. The Phillies lost the game—and the $10,000.

V

Outrageous

75 | AN INCREDIBLE CASE OF FAN DEVOTION

The Tigers were trailing by one run in the eleventh inning of a crucial game. Detroit had runners at first and third bases while J. D. Reed, an anxious fan at Briggs Stadium, bit his nails, hoping for the home team to score.

Suddenly, the umpire stopped the game, walked toward the stands, and did something rarely seen at a Major League game. The arbiter announced, "Is there a J. D. Reed in the stands?"

Stunned by the umpire's query, Reed raised his arm, signaling that J. D. was, in fact, there watching the contest.

"Sir," the man in blue told Reed, "you are needed at home immediately. Your house is on fire!"

Reed digested the warning for a few seconds and shouted back, "Let the darn thing burn. I gotta see the end of this game."

76 | THE REMARKABLE BIRD IN CASEY'S HAT

Defenders of legendary player-manager Casey Stengel argue that his accomplishments far outweigh his capers on and off the field. They point to his World Series triumphs with the Yankees as proof positive that he was a managerial magician. However, Stengel's critics assert that the "Old Professor" performed too many clownish acts that tarnished his image. Easily the most bizarre of this genre was a seemingly magical feat he pulled off as a member of the Pirates after being dealt to Pittsburgh by the Brooklyn Dodgers, with whom he had been a fan favorite.

On Stengel's first visit to Flatbush following the trade, Casey wanted to show his appreciation to the Ebbets Field faithful for their passionate support of his efforts. As it happened, when Stengel took his first turn at bat in the top of the second inning, the fans gave him a standing ovation.

Ever grateful for the support, Casey turned to the grandstand, bowed, and removed his cap in salute to the audience. At first, the crowd roared its approval, but suddenly, it seemed that every patron got a momentary case of lockjaw when they noticed a real, *live* bird perched on top of Stengel's head. (It was believed to be a starling, a bird often seen in Brooklyn.) As Ole Case began replacing the cap, his fine, feathered friend took off, circled the bases and was last seen winging its way west toward Prospect Park and, perhaps, eventually Pennsylvania.

As the bird disappeared, thousands of fans applauded again but few ever learned how the bird emerged in the first place from Stengel's scalp. Naturally, Casey—never at a loss for words—explained.

When he sauntered out to right field in the bottom of the first inning, he noticed an injured bird near the scoreboard. Fearing that he might step on the feathered one, Casey simply placed it under his cap and proceeded to focus on the game at hand. That is, until the grand gesture of applause from Brooklyn fans.

Those who knew Stengel best insisted that it was as flighty as Casey ever got.

As for the bird, it was the first and last starring role for the starling.

77 | BENCHED BECAUSE OF SPELLING PROBLEMS

Oscar Roettger was a pretty fair outfielfer for the Brooklyn Dodgers

Talented or not, Roettger got benched one day because his manager, "Uncle" Wilbert Robinson, had a forgetful moment when handing in his starting lineup.

Robbie's plan was to put Roettger in right field, but he got a mental block and couldn't spell Oscar's last name.

The Dodgers manager turned to the player sitting next to him in the dugout. "How do you spell Oscar's last name?" pleaded Robinson. The player shook his head—he didn't know.

"To Hell with it," snapped Uncle Robbie, "I'm benching him and putting Dick Cox in right!"

Which he did!

78 | HOW A BLEACHERS SPECTATOR CHANGED PITCHERS FOR THE DODGERS

A s baseball fans go, Hilda Chester was in a league of her own.

From the late 1930s to the departure of the Dodgers from Brooklyn in 1957, Chester sat in the same center field bleachers seat at Ebbets Field, rarely missing a game featuring "Dem Bums," as her lovable Brooks were called.

Hilda never attended a game without two items: 1. a large cowbell, which could be heard from her seat to home plate and; 2. a banner proclaiming, "Hilda Is Here," as if any spectator had to be advised of that fact.

Among her other attributes, Chester studied baseball as assiduously as Dodgers manager Leo (The Lip) Durocher and rarely withheld her opinions. However, one fateful day Hilda's view of strategy took a strange turn away from Durocher's and, in turn, got center field Pistol Pete Reiser into hot water with his skipper.

The episode unfolded while the Dodgers and Cardinals were battling for first place during a torrid run for the 1941 National League pennant. Durocher had his ace Whitlow Wyatt on the mound while Cards manager Billy Southworth went with his best, Morton Cooper. Dodgers president Larry MacPhail was watching the game from his box behind the home dugout.

Like George Steinbrenner of a later era, MacPhail was a hard-drinking extrovert who frequently enraged his manager by dictating strategy to Durocher. But this time the dictation was to come from a different direction.

Despite the fact that it was a scoreless battle, Hilda sensed that Wyatt's arm was faltering. It bothered her to the point that she grabbed a pencil and scribbled a note meant for Durocher: WYATT IS LOSING IT; TAKE HIM OUT; PUT CASEY IN.

At the time Hugh Casey was the National League's best relief pitcher and figured to save the game if, in fact, Wyatt was slipping. While the Cardinals were still at bat, Chester dropped her note over the side of the bleachers and on to the center field grass. Immediately noticing the message with a cover line—FOR LEO—Reiser pocketed the paper until the inning ended and he headed for dugout. Before stepping down, Pistol Pete exchanged a few words with MacPhail and then handed the note to his manager, who read it and made the mistake of the day.

Durocher thought the note was another bit of bad advice from MacPhail. In fact Leo thought the advice was so misinformed that he decided to embarrass his boss by pulling Wyatt, which he did. Sure enough, just as the Lip had figured, Casey got whacked around something awful, but the Dodgers still managed to eke out a win.

Meanwhile, Reiser entered the clubhouse, delighted with the victory until Durocher confronted him head to head. "Tell MacPhail that this is the last time I'm ever gonna do what he tells me when it comes to changing pitchers and Larry knows what he can do with his note."

Wondering what the heck was going on, Pistol Pete immediately shot back that MacPhail had nothing to do with the pitching change. Still furious, Leo demanded, "Then, who gave you that note?"

"Oh, Skipper," Reiser explained, "I forgot to tell you; it came from Hilda Chester up in the bleachers."

Durocher worked hard to keep from exploding and finally remarked, "And you're gonna have me take out pitchers on the request of some dame in the cheap seats?"

Then a pause: "Pete, please don't ever do that again."

Liking his job more than he liked Hilda Chester, Reiser obliged.

79 | THREE MEN ON THIRD—HOW CAN THAT HAPPEN?

In retrospect, it seems like a surrealistic scene that could have emerged from an Abbott and Costello farcical film about diamond madness in Brooklyn, but this scene actually took place in real life.

During a Brooklyn Dodgers batting spree against the Boston Braves, three of the Brooks—Dazzy Vance, Chick Fewster, and Babe Herman—all wound up on third base for one of the all-time diamond faux pas.

Actually this inadvertent burlesque of baseball-running began innocently enough as Willie (Uncle Robbie) Robinson's Dodgers filled the bases with one out at Ebbets Field. The batter was Herman, while Hank DeBerry occupied third, Fewster was on second, and Vance led off first base.

No slouch at the plate, Herman sizzled a drive to right field that easily sent DeBerry home. Somehow, Vance got the impression that the ball might be caught, so he held up momentarily just to be sure. After a long pause, the slow-footed Vance headed toward third where coach Mickey O'Neil waved him home. Dazzy at first obeyed the command but, half-way to the plate, suffered second thoughts about the wisdom of the move and hustled back to third.

So far so good; but not for long.

Fewster, who had been on first, wanted to make the most of Herman's blast thought it would be a breeze to reach third and slowed down. By contrast, the ever-hustling Herman had put his head down attempting to break the sixty-yard-dash record on a baseball diamond. Babe *passed* Fewster, arriving at third a couple of steps ahead of his teammate.

Imagine their surprise—not to mention Uncle Robbie's and that of a few thousand fans—when Vance, Herman, and Fewster realized that they were occupying the same hot corner. Boston's third baseman put the tag on Fewster while Herman got the message and tried to hustle toward second out of harm's way.

Too late. The Babe was tagged out, and the result of the trio on third was actually a double play. This blunder of Brooklyn blunders inspired many a quaint quip, starting with manager Robinson, who remarked to reporters, "It's the first time those three guys got together all season."

Vaudevillians on the stage of Brooklyn's Loew's Orpheum Theater followed up with a blackout scene that went like this:

First vaudevillian, listening to a Dodgers game on the radio: "Hey, Jack, I hear that the Dodgers have three men on base."

Second vaudevillian: "Which base?"

80 | THE AMAZING AERIAL BASEBALL–GRAPEFRUIT TRICK

When Casey Stengel and Willie Robinson were teammates on the 1916 Brooklyn Dodgers, the team held training camp at Daytona Beach, Florida. At that time, Ruth Law, one of the first female pilots in America, was practicing a publicity stunt.

Ms. Law would take her plane to a height of about one thousand feet and drop golf balls into the Daytona Beach sand. Ruth's stunt was meant to demonstrate the terrific force of gravity. When Stengel heard about Ruth's golf ball flight of fancy, he suggested an even better gimmick. Casey suggested that Law drop a baseball from her plane and have the Brooks' outstanding catcher, Robinson, camp underneath and catch it in his big mitt.

It was argued that a thousand feet was a bit too high, but dropping a baseball from four hundred feet in the air was more like it, so the stage was set for this unusual challenge. Ruth was accompanied in the plane by the Dodgers trainer, Frank Kelly, who would be the ball tosser; that is, if everything was on the up and up—which it was not.

As teammates and onlookers awaited the stunt, the ever-playful Stengel urged Kelly to pack a Florida grapefruit in his satchel along with the baseball. "Hold on to the ball," ordered Stengel, "and toss the grapefruit."

Kelly followed Casey's advice, and as the plane zoomed toward home plate, the trainer leaned out of the open cockpit and flung the grapefruit into the air. Meanwhile, Robinson stood behind the plate watching what looked like an oversized baseball plummeting toward his outstretched arms.

Alas, the grapefruit went through Robinsons's left mitt and right hand, smacking Robbie's chest and knocking him for a loop over home plate. Not certain what had hit him, the catcher screamed, "It split my chest—I'm bleeding to death."

As one reporter put it, "The players around Uncle Robbie were closer to death than he was—from hysterical convulsions."

81 | THE MOST INCREDIBLE START TO A PITCHING SEASON

Talk about getting off on the right foot, no pitcher could top what Rube Marquard did on the mound for the New York Giants in 1912. With an opening win over Brooklyn (18–3), Marquard became the most feared pitcher in baseball. By July 4, 1912, he had tallied a 19–0 record, the longest winning streak in a single season.

One reason for Marquard's success was the sensational hitting displayed by his teammates. During the nineteen-game streak, the Giants outscored their opponents, 129–49, averaging almost seven runs per game. Marquard's streak included only one shutout, and it wasn't until his thirteenth win that he had to struggle, his team ahead only by one run.

His most dramatic victory was the nineteenth, a 2–1 triumph over Brooklyn. His pitching opponent was Napoleon Rucker, who allowed four Giants hits. One of New York's runs came as a result of a dropped pop-up by Bert Tooley, Brooklyn's shortstop. Brooklyn threatened in the ninth inning with the winning runners on base and one out, but Marquard struck out heavy-hitting Zach Wheat and ended the game with a fly ball out. Rube's luck ran out on July 9 at Wrigley Field in Chicago. The Chicago Cubs routed Marquard and the Giants, 7–2. From then on, Rube faltered and ran up a dismal 7–11 win-loss mark for the rest of the season.

82 | WRITING BASEBALL'S BOBBY THOMSON INTO A NON-BASEBALL MOVIE SCRIPT

Best known for his histrionics at bat for the New York Giants, Bobby Thomson got mentioned in a major Metro Goldwyn Mayor film in 1953.

The movie was called *Mogambo*. In the flick, Grace Kelly, responding to Clark Gable's identification of a group of scurrying animals as "Thomson's gazelles," asks: "Who is this man, Thomson, that gazelles should be called after him?"

Ava Gardner, in jealous pursuit of Gable's charms, and definitely another kind of lady, answers sardonically: "He's a third baseman for the Giants who hit a home run against the Dodgers, once."

According to experts on films, this could be the closest adherence to baseball fact ever achieved in a Hollywood production. "Baseball movies," wrote the late film critic Paul Ringe, "traditionally have been viewed with suspicion by baseball fans. But *Mogambo* did justice to both Bobby Thomson and Gazelles."

Interestingly, baseball themes go as far back as silent movies. Two of the best silent films about baseball include *How the Office Boy Saw the Ballgame* (1906) and *Bush Leaguer* (1917).

83 | HOW LEGENDARY AFRICAN AMERICAN CATCHER JOSH GIBSON TURNED A HOME RUN INTO A DOUBLE

The pity of it all is that Josh Gibson's timing was bad. Had he been born twenty years later there's no question that the legendary African American catcher would have excelled in Major League Baseball; yes, he was that good.

Many a seasoned baseball critic has lumped Gibson on to the same starry level as Roy Campanella, Bill Dickey, and Yogi Berra, among many Hall of Fame backstops. Josh was a power hitter in the Babe Ruth tradition, a crafty catcher, and an all-round star, as was a later African American catcher, Campanella, was with the Brooklyn Dodgers.

In addition, Gibson was a bit of a clown, and his sense of humor—not to mention sense of worth—was demonstrated one Sunday afternoon during the early 1940s when Josh's Homestead (Pittsburgh) Grays visited the Bushwicks at their home field, Dexter Park located smack on the Brooklyn (Cypress Hills)-Queens (Woodhaven) border.

Long regarded as the best semipro team in America, the Bushwicks' ballpark was abnormal in its geography. Right field was rather normal in that it had a fence more than three hundred feet out to the foul line and there was a scoreboard in right-center field. But from dead-center to left field there was a ten-foot hill on which D-E-X-T-E-R P-A-R-K was spelled out with oversized clam shells. And just beyond the hill was a picnic grounds.

I was sitting in the third base grandstands when Gibson poled the longest line drive I have ever seen. It measured about five hundred feet, landing on the flat plain of the picnic ground and by all rights should have been a home run.

Should have been.

But on this hot summer day, Josh thought otherwise, and when he reached second base Gibson put on the brakes and simply sat down on the bag as if it was his private chaise lounge from which he could watch the Bushwicks' center fielder retrieve the ball and relay it to the infield.

Josh's point was illustrated without a word being spoken. He and everyone else *knew* it was a home run; he had made his point. Now he was just too tired to clear the bases so, for this precious moment, a two-bagger would do.

And it did—without a complaint from either side of the Brooklyn-Queens border.

HOW AN INCREDIBLY DISSONANT MUSICAL GROUP HAD THE LONGEST-RUNNING RECORD AT A BALLPARK

84

As former Brooklyn Dodgers manager Leo Durocher once said, "It could only happen at Ebbets Field."

In this case, it was the formation of the zany musical combination that, by critical standards, should never have lasted more than one game. But, the Dodgers Sym-Phony Band survived two decades at the Brooklyn stadium.

At each game, the Sym-Phony occupied Section 8, Row 1, Seats 1 through 7 at the ballpark and never failed to amuse friend and foe alike. Irving Rudd, who was the Dodgers' publicist during the halcyon days on the Sym-Phony, once described them thusly:

"They had a dual purpose: to amuse the crowd at the ballpark and to harass opposing players. There was JoJo Delio on the snare drum, and Brother Lou Soriano belted the bass drum and was the Sym-Phony conductor. There was Patty George, Jerry Martin, and Joe Zollo and his son Frank.

"The umpires, when they first appeared on the field to start a ball game, got the musical razz, 'Three Blind Mice.' When a fourth umpire was added routinely to every game, the boys were stumped. Complained Brother Lou, 'We can't help it. We cannot come up with the fourth mouse.' They used to toot and drum an opposing batsman, especially if he struck out, back to his dugout with a rhythmic cadence and waited until the player sat down, at which time they blared forth with a big chord. If it took a long time for the player to sit down, the Sym-Phony waited a long time, but the big blare always came as soon as the flannel trousers touched the bench.

"Back in July 1951, Local 802 of the American Federation of Musicians questioned the amateur standing of the Brooklyn Dodgers' Sym-Phony Band and threatened to throw a picket line around Ebbets Field. The Dodgers thereupon scheduled a Musical Unappreciation night. Admittance was free as long as you brought a musical instrument. And so they came, more than thirty thousand strong, with harmonicas, drums, kazoos, and every conceivable type of portable instrument including— yes!—even two pianos, which were brought into the rotunda at the main entrance.

"What a night for music! The weird noises unleashed by the capacity crowd of roof-raisers must have traumatized music lovers for miles around."

85 | GAME CALLED ON ACCOUNT OF—GET THIS!—A HURRICANE

Nowadays, it takes an awful lot of downpour to cause a Major League Baseball game to be cancelled, but at least once in the game's history, a contest was called on account of a *hurricane*.

On September 21, 1938, a killer hurricane spread its fury over New England. The Boston Bees (prior to 1936 and after 1940, they were known as the Boston Braves) were entertaining the St. Louis Cardinals for a doubleheader. During the second game, winds blew across the field with terrifying velocity. Umpire Beans Reardon decided he had better call the game because of the impending hurricane. And just what prompted Reardon's historic move? The umpire decided that something should be done when *fly balls to center field were being caught in foul territory by catcher Al Lopez!*

86 | WHICH TEAM WAS RESPONSIBLE FOR BASEBALL'S LONGEST WINNING STREAK, YET FINISHED FOURTH?

If winning streaks could be equated with winning a pennant, the 1916 New York Giants would have topped the National League.

Not only did manager John McGraw's team win at their home Polo Grounds in Harlem, but they also did extraordinarily well on the road.

The overall skein totaled twenty-six undefeated games, of which seventeen straight were accomplished on the road.

Steel-tongued McGraw and his team had come off a disappointing last-place finish in 1915 and was determined to make amends for their rooters in the new season. McGraw, the Captain Bligh of baseball, drove the team unmercifully to seventeen consecutive road victories—an all-time record—but that still did not appease the bench boss.

Midseason, he decided that many of his veterans had to be traded, and he dealt away such notables as pitcher Christy Mathewson and outfielder Eddie Roush.

On September 7, 1916, the Giants defeated Brooklyn and suddenly became a team possessed. A day later, they met Philadelphia in a doubleheader. Poll Perritt, who had won the first game for the Giants on the mound, pleaded with McGraw

to pitch the second game after having been viciously needled by the Phillies.

Demanding of his manager, "Let me beat those bums again," Perrit started the second game and came through with a four-hit shutout. Now the streak was for real.

By September 30, 1916, the Giants' undefeated streak had reached twenty-five games. Their next opponent—in a doubleheader—was the Boston Braves. McGraw's men won the opening game, lengthening their streak to twenty-six, but lost the second match and ended their remarkable streak that had lasted from September 7 through September 30.

Despite McGraw's ranting and raving, the Giants finished nowhere near the top of the National League. However, they did enter the record books, and for that, they will long be remembered.

87 | UNBELIEVABLY, THREE MAJOR LEAGUE TEAMS OPPOSED EACH OTHER IN THE SAME GAME

The circumstances had to be unusual for such an event to take place, but on one afternoon in Manhattan, the Brooklyn Dodgers, New York Yankees, and New York Giants played each other on the same field.

It happened on June 26, 1944, at the Polo Grounds in New York. The game was staged as a gimmick to raise money for the United States war bonds during World War II.

Each team played successive innings against the other two, and then sat out for an inning. The six-inning exhibition proved a huge success, drawing more than fifty thousand fans.

The Dodgers hold the distinction of beating two teams in one game, 5–1–0.

The line score for the game:

Brooklyn Dodgers	1	2	0	0	0	2	5
New York Yankees	0	0	0	0	0	1	1
New York Giants	0	0	0	0	0	0	0

THE EXTRAORDINARY CIRCUMSTANCES THAT FORCED A MANAGER TO PULL HIS ACCLAIMED OUTFIELDER IN THE MIDDLE OF GAME SEVEN OF THE WORLD SERIES

88

It was Game Seven of the 1934 World Series between the St. Louis Cardinals and Detroit Tigers, in Detroit.

The visiting Cardinals put up seven runs in the third inning and showed no signs of letting up.

By the end of the fifth inning, the Cards led 11–0 and the Tiger fans were growing increasingly angry.

That's when things got interesting.

In the top of the sixth inning, Joe "Ducky" Medwick, the .319-hitting St. Louis left fielder, hit a triple—his first of the Series—and finished the play by sliding hard into third baseman Marv Owen.

Medwick's triple was not surprising, since he had smacked eighteen to lead the National League in three-baggers that year. But it was the last straw for the Tigers fans, particularly when Joe wrestled briefly with Owen in an effort to beat the tag and get to his feet. Briggs Stadium was in an uproar when the Cardinals finally were retired, still leading 11–0.

When Medwick ran out to left field to start the bottom of the sixth, he was pelted with garbage, bottles, fruit, and assorted debris. To avoid injury, Medwick wandered off to second base while the groundskeeper cleared off the field.

When Ducky returned, the fans bombarded him again, this time with increased vigor. Baseball Commissioner Kenesaw Mountain Landis summoned St. Louis manager Frankie Frisch and ordered Medwick's removal from the game.

Medwick reluctantly departed in favor of Chick Fullis. The Cardinals won, 11–0, to take the Series in seven games.

89 | WHY DID A GAME-WINNING GRAND SLAM IN THE BOTTOM OF THE NINTH GET CALLED BACK?

On April 10, 1976, the visiting New York Yankees were leading the Milwaukee Brewers, 9–6. In the bottom of the ninth inning, the Brewers loaded the bases, and Don Money stepped up to the plate.

Yankee ace reliever Sparky Lyle then served up a fat pitch, which Money crushed into the right field bleachers, for what appeared to be a game-winning home run.

The fans in Milwaukee went into a frenzy. But this short-lived party was about to come to a screeching halt.

First base umpire, Bill McKean, began consulting with his fellow umpires. As it turned out, before the pitch, Yankee manager Billy Martin was yelling instructions to Lyle, but the pitcher was unable to hear them over the roar of the Milwaukee crowd.

However, Chris Chambliss, the Yankees' first baseman, had heard Martin and quietly asked umpire McKean for a timeout so he could relay the word to Lyle.

McKean called for a timeout, but Lyle, still not hearing a thing, pitched to Money. Ultimately, blame for the faux pas was charged to the screaming Milwaukee fans.

Umpire McKean ordered the home run canceled, Lyle served another pitch to Money and struck him out, and the Yankees eventually won, 9–7.

90 | AN INCREDIBLE MURDER BECAUSE OF BASEBALL PASSION

On a summer night in 1938, a murder took place because of passionate Dodgers fans, which could only happen in Brooklyn.

Patty Diamond's bar on Ninth Street and Seventh Avenue in the Park Slope section of the borough was packed with its usual complement of Ebbets Field rooters. One of the regulars, Robert Joyce, was a bit more passionate about Dem Bums than the other beer-guzzlers.

Pat Diamond's son, Bill, happened to be tending bar and was, himself, a Brooks fan but had been disappointed in their recent losing streak. Talking to a customer named Frank Krug, visiting from Albany, New York, Bill mentioned to Frank, "Whoever called the Dodgers bums was right."

To which Krug nodded agreement and then added the deathless words, "It takes the Giants to show them up as bums too."

Unfortunately, Joyce happened to overhear the exchange and felt obliged to stick his two cents into the discussion. "Shut up," demanded Joyce. "Lay off the Dodgers."

Those witness to the growing debate insist that Krug then added that only a jerk would be a Dodgers fan.

With that, the increasingly enraged Joyce bolted from the bar, leaving his beer unattended, only to return moments later with additional baggage: a loaded pistol.

Confronting the astonished Krug, Joyce then added the clincher: "A jerk. I'll show you who's a jerk."

Joyce's first shot went through Krug's head. And if that didn't punctuate the lecture, the still-furious Dodgers fan turned on Bill Diamond and got him in the stomach.

Within minutes, the police arrived to find a sobbing gun-slinger who insisted that he did not mean to kill Krug or wound Diamond.

It was just, "That I had taken all I could about the Dodgers!"

Or, as author David W. McCullough noted in his book, *Brooklyn...And How It Got That Way*, "It was an archetypical Brooklyn crime in a typical Brooklyn bar."

91 | A WORLD SERIES-WINNING TEAM WITH AN ARRESTING COLLECTION OF NICKNAMES AND TWO COOPERS

The team was the 1942 World Series-winning St. Louis Cardinals.

To start with, the Redbirds had some of the neatest nicknames in baseball. They included Stan "The Man" Musial, Enos "Country" Slaughter, and Harry "The Hat" Walker, as well as Frank A. J. "Creepy" Crespi, who played alongside John "Hippety" Hopp, George "Righty" Kurowski, and Marty "Slats" Marion.

In addition, manager Billy Southwuth's team also had a Coaker and two Coopers. Coaker Triplett played the left field position.

The Coopers comprised the Cardinals' famed pitcher-catcher brother act of Morton and Walker Cooper.

Coaker Triplett (along with Stan "The Man" Musial, Enos "Country" Slaughter, and Harry "The Hat" Walker) played in the St. Louis outfield when the Cards defeated the New York Yankees, four games to one.

92 | THREE-FOR-THREE, THE REGGIE JACKSON WAY

They didn't call him Mister October for nothing.

Reggie Jackson emerged as one of the most electrifying clutch hitters in baseball annals. And there are many exhibits that prove the point. One of the best took place on October 18, 1977, in Game Six of the 1977 World Series.

In 1967, it became evident to all that he possessed an obsession to crush baseballs. And he did so with the only weapon at his disposal, his bat, driving the ball further and further away from the plate with each air-shattering swing.

Reggie Jackson joined the Yankees before the 1976 season. He signed a multiyear contract worth $2.6 million, making him the highest-paid player in baseball history.

Jackson said, "I didn't come to New York to be a star. I brought my star with me."

The Yankees beat the Kansas City Royals in the 1977 championship series, three games to two, but Jackson could only muster one hit in his fifteen at bats during the first four games. He was benched for Game Five of the championship series. There were now several questions about the fate of Jackson. Will he play in the World Series?

Billy Martin started Jackson in the first two games. Jackson got a bloop single in his first plate appearance. That was the only hit he got in the first two games. The Yankees were able to win the first game against the Dodgers, but did not win the second game before winning two of the next three games.

The Yankees were now leading the Series three to two heading into Game Six at Yankee Stadium. Jackson was leading the charge with six hits in his last seventeen plate appearances. Reggie always had a mountain of confidence in his ability, but nobody else could believe just how great he could be.

For on that night of October 18, 1977, Reggie Jackson, with a component of embellishment in his style, was to make baseball history. He was to do it on the stage "the Sultan of Swat" made famous, Yankee Stadium, appropriately called "The House that Ruth Built."

In his first at bat, Jackson worked a walk. He was driven in that inning by Chris Chambliss' home run to tie the game at two. Jackson's next at bat came in the fourth inning. The Dodgers took the lead 3–2 earlier in the game. With the Yankee captain, Thurman Munson, on first base, Jackson smashed the first pitch he saw deep into the right field bleachers. The Yankees now led 4–3.

Jackson was determined to make history that night. He came to the plate for a third time, facing one of the Dodgers relief pitchers, Elias Sosa. Jackson swung at the first pitch again and hammered it to the right field stands. Another two-run homer for Jackson, and the Yankees now led 7–3.

The fans were chanting, "REG-GIE! REG-GIE! REG-GIE!

Reggie Jackson came up to the plate again in the eighth inning. The fans were on their feet. Charlie Hough came in for the Dodgers to pitch. These two had faced each other one other time during the Series, in Game Three. Hough was able to strike out Reggie on his devastating knuckleball.

Jackson came to life like a clockwork toy, swinging that glorious swing of his. On the first pitch once again, Reggie pulverized the ball to deep center field, 450 feet away, a blast that dwarfed his other two by comparison. Jackson stood at the plate admiring his handiwork and welcoming the eruption by Yankees fans.

Dodgers manager Tommy Lasorda called it "The greatest single performance I've ever seen." Not only did Jackson tie Ruth's record of three home runs in a World Series game, but he also did it on three consecutive pitches.

After a heroic effort in Game Six, he was known as "Mister October" from then on. During the 1977 Fall Classic, Jackson set records for most home runs in one Series with five, most runs with ten, and most total bases with twenty-five.

93 | HARVEY HADDIX'S IMPERFECT PERFECT GAME

Sometimes in baseball, you can lie with statistics. Exhibit A had to be a game played on May 26, 1959.

Pittsburgh pitcher Harvey Haddix faced twenty-seven Milwaukee Braves batters, and twenty-seven went down without a hit.

How about Exhibit B, accomplish that same day: Haddix went twelve perfect innings, sending down thirty-six Milwaukee batters in a row.

And still he lost the perfecto, no-hitter, and the game in the thirteenth inning.

Whoever said baseball is fair? The man who would come to be known as "Hard Luck Harvey" certainly had none that night–it was an error by third baseman Don Hoak that broke up the perfect game and ultimately led to Haddix's undoing. His Pirates lost 1–0. The run was unearned.

But who won and who lost on that fateful night is really unimportant when considering the significance of Haddix's performance. Haddix is the only man in the history of baseball to throw more than nine perfect innings—Pedro Martinez was perfect when he took the mound for the tenth in 1995, but batter number twenty-eight broke it up.

In the modern era, thirteen pitchers carried no-hitters—not perfect games—into extra innings, but only two lasted past the tenth and none past the eleventh.

The longest officially recognized no-no went ten innings—it's been done three times, but only once since 1920. Haddix's performance stands alone—the Ferdinand Magellan of games pitched—for on that night, he navigated waters no pitcher before, and none since, has ever come close to.

Making Haddix's performance all the more astonishing is due to the team he faced that night. The first-place Braves were fresh off appearing in consecutive World Series and would lead the league in home runs in 1959.

The southpaw Haddix faced a lineup featuring the likes of twenty-five-year-old Hank Aaron, who at first pitch was hitting a robust .453—Hammerin' Hank would hit a career-best .355 in 1959, along with his standard thirty-nine home runs—Hall-of-Famer Eddie Mathews, who finished second in MVP voting and hit forty-six long balls, and the lesser-known, but still formidable, Joe Adcock, a man who slugged over three hundred homers in his career.

All told, Haddix that day faced a lineup featuring the two men who would combine to lead baseball in two-thirds of the vaunted Triple Crown categories in 1959: batting average (Aaron) and home runs (Mathews).

Comically, Hard Luck Harvey didn't even realize he had a perfect game going. Haddix was dealing with a bad cold all night long, and his head was a bit foggy—from either the cold or the lozenges he was devouring between innings. He was aware he was throwing a no-hitter, but he thought he had issued a free pass earlier in the game. In reality, Haddix's control was so superb that he only threw ball three once all night—in the first inning to Eddie Mathews. The lefty would later quip: "I could have put a cup on either corner of the plate and hit it."

Haddix's dominance was so utter and complete that there was nary a hard hit ball until the fateful thirteenth. A then relatively unknown second baseman named Bill Mazeroski would later say: "Usually you have one or two great or spectacular defensive plays in these no-hitters. Not that night. It was the easiest game I ever played in."

Haddix, a change-speeds, keep-'em-off-balance type of pitcher throughout his career, elected to use just two pitches that night—fastball and slider. If you were a Milwaukee Brave, and you guessed what was coming, you had a fifty-fifty shot of being right…at least under normal circumstances, that is.

In reality, no guesswork was needed—Braves hitters knew exactly what was coming—because a pair of binoculars trained on catcher Smoky Burgess had enabled the Milwaukee bullpen to steal the signs. A towel on the shoulder of a reliever signaled breaking ball; no towel meant fastball. All the batters, but Hank Aaron, took the signals.

We can quibble all day about whether knowing what's coming helps a hitter—some, like Aaron most likely, would say it doesn't—but when eight of nine guys in a lineup know exactly what's being served up for twelve innings and still can't touch it—then it becomes clear there's something special going on with the man on the mound that night, and for Haddix, there certainly was.

Maybe it's because Haddix's masterpiece isn't officially recognized as a perfect game, or maybe it has something to do with the fact that Haddix himself is not a brand name (he was a solid—not spectacular—pitcher), but in the pantheon of remarkable games, Haddix's gem is often overlooked. Poll a hundred baseball fans and ask them all if they know who Harvey Haddix is—I'd be willing to wager that half, if not even more, have never heard of the man.

In the long history of baseball, there's not many things left that have only been done once. Hitting sixty home runs was supposed to be impossible—it's been done eight times—hitting seventy was unconscionable—it's happened twice—yet Haddix's twelve perfect innings remain untouched and unchallenged. Perhaps Haddix put it best, when asked about a 1991 rule change that took his performance off the list of perfect games: "It's OK. I know what I did." Regardless of what the record book says and what people remember, on that night, Harvey Haddix was imperfectly perfect.

94 | SKEPTICS BEWARE—A DOUBLE-NO-HITTER

Talk about defying credulity, how about a pair of pitchers facing each other and each tossing a no-hitter?

The hurlers were Jim Vaughn of the Chicago Cubs, a left-hander, and Fred Toney, a big Cincinnati Red right-hander.

According to authors Joe Reichler and Ben Olan, who wrote *Baseball's Unforgettable Games*, the contest on May 2, 1917, featured "baseball's greatest pitching duel."

What gives that statement credence is the fact that Toney pitched ten hitless innings, while Vaughn did likewise for nine innings before giving up a run in the tenth.

The venue was Wrigley Field, then called Weeghman Park, in Chicago. After the pitchers had retired a combined fifty-four batters without surrendering a hit, Larry Kropf of the Cincinnati Reds got the first base-knock of the game. He hit a screaming line drive to right field. Following Kropf's hit, there were two errors that cost Toney and Chicago the game.

Chicago had one last chance in the bottom of the tenth inning. After Vaughn struck out the first two batters, Fred Merkle came to the plate. He hit a towering drive to deep left field that looked to be the game-tying home run, but at the last moment, Cuban left fielder Emanuel Cueto caught the ball with his back to the bleachers.

The Reds went on to win the pitching duel 1–0.

95 | TAKE ME OUT TO THE BRAWL GAME—AT THE COPA

Baseball's most famous brawl didn't even take place on the diamond.

It took place on May 16, 1957, at what then was New York's most famous night club, the Copacabana at 10 East 60th Street in Manhattan.

The clash took place on a festive occasion, Billy Martin's twenty-ninth birthday.

A superb infield and clutch hitter for the Yankees, Martin was even more notorious for his fistfights. He battled such opponents as Boston's Jimmy Piersall, St. Louis' Clint Courtney, and the Cubs' Jim Brewer.

But these were small potatoes compared to the Copa bout, which was witnessed by several teammates, including Mickey Mantle, Yogi Berra, Hank Bauer, Gil McDougal, and Johnny Kucks.

You better believe that the hell-raisers had downed more than a few whiskeys to toast Billy's fete. Among the celebrants was Copa's star of the show, Sammy Davis Jr., a popular singer and comic of that era.

No less boisterous at the next table was a nineteen-member New Jersey bowling team called the Republicans, along with their kegging wives.

What followed was something a bit worse than a Pier 6 brawl.

According to the Yankees, the culprit was Edwin Jones, a delicatessen owner and prominent member of the bowlers contingent. The Bombers insisted that Jones showered a range of insults at Davis while he was trying to perform.

When "Husky" Hank Bauer of the Yanks urged the bowlers to pipe down, they responded with another barrage of unkind words about Davis.

That did it. As Jim Reisler chronicled in his book, *Babe Ruth Slept Here: The Baseball Landmarks of New York City*, all hell broke loose.

"What happened next was a tabloid headline writer's dream as Yankees and bowlers fell, scuffling and fighting to the floor in front of the stage," wrote Reisler.

A body flew into the coatroom and policemen flooded the club in front of the Yankees' table #11.

"Jones paid for his alleged remark, ending up with a broken nose, a fractured jaw, and a concussion. Bauer, hitting .203 at the time, took most of the heat for striking Jones, but denied it. 'Hit him?' he asked. "I haven't hit anybody all year.' The ballplayers claimed it was the nightclub bouncer who inflicted most of the damage."

The brouhaha was grist for the media's mill. Every newspaper headlined the fight, especially since Bauer was arrested for assault.

Reisler explained, "Martin died in 1989 from injuries sustained while driving intoxicated in upstate New York. He is buried in Gate of Heaven Cemetery in Hawthorne, an infield-peg of a distance from the grave of Babe Ruth."

96 | THE GREATEST BASE-BRAWL RIVALRY

Historians can find several incidents over the past century that have inspired the white-heat hatred between the New York Yankees and Boston Red Sox. The fierce enmity extended long ago between the respective supporters of each distinguished nine.

What's more, the rivalry extends far beyond Babe Ruth's move from Beantown to Broadway. And nothing demonstrates the intercity dislike more than brawls that have erupted on their respective diamonds.

One only has to check out the events of May 1938 at Yankee Stadium as Exhibit A.

Boston left-hander, Archie McKain, had been throwing too close to Jake Powell, a Yankee outfielder. Powell rushed to the mound but never made it.

Red Sox shortstop Joe Cronin intercepted Powell and started swinging in defense of McKain. Cronin, however, was not announced as a "pinch hitter" before cooler heads prevailed.

Fenway Park was the scene of another Sox-Yanks clash, in 1952. Only this time, Billy Martin of the Bronx Bombers and Jimmy Piersall of the Red Sox couldn't wait for the game to begin. They went at it before the players even took the field.

Beanballs played a role in Yanks-Sox Brawl III, at Yankee Stadium in 1967.

In the course of the game, New York hurler Thad Tillotson hit Boston third baseman Joe Foy with a pitch. Retribution came in the form of a Jim Lonborg fastball. The Yankees' bench emptied and a brouhaha ensued.

The main bout took place between Boston's Rico Petrocelli and the Yankees' Joe Pepitone.

Home plate at Fenway was transformed into another war zone in 1973, all because Gene Michael of the Yankees missed a suicide squeeze bunt.

The runner from third, Thurman Munson, a catcher by trade, saw Carleton Fisk, Boston's pride of home plate, catch the ball and braced himself for a collision between the two best young catchers in the American League.

Munson was ready too—and with elbows way up. BANG!

Fisk absorbed the full impact of Munson's 188 pounds, landed on his American Express card, and came up swinging.

Both Munson and Michael then attacked Fisk, leaving him with a bruised eye and a scratched face.

"The Yankees and Red Sox have played this way since baseball was invented," said Fisk. "I must admit we get out there against them with a lot of intensity. Sometimes we get carried away a little." On a warm Thursday night in May 1976, Boston's flaky left-handed pitcher, Bill Lee, almost had to be carried away himself, following a bench-clearing brawl with the rival New Yorkers in the refurbished Yankee Stadium.

The defending American League champs trailed the first-place Yankees by six games as the two clubs began a four-game weekend series.

In the bottom half of the sixth, New York was threatening to add to its precarious 1–0 lead, with Lou Piniella on second base and Graig Nettles on first. The batter, Otto Velez, lined a Lee fast-ball into right field.

Dwight Evans, who earlier had thrown out Fred Stanley at home plate, again faced the challenge of retiring a base runner at home.

As the medium-fast Piniella chugged around third base with the green light from coach Dick Howser, the charging Evans scooped up the ball, reared back, and fired an accurate one-hop throw to catcher Fisk.

The Sox's talented backstop received the skidding throw on the first base side of the plate, turned on his knees to meet the sliding Yankee runner, and tagged him out. But it didn't end there.

Piniella thought the ball had been jarred loose by the collision and tried desperately to kick it away so that umpire Terry Cooney would see it.

But instead of the ball, Piniella inadvertently kicked Fisk.

Having suffered several painful groin injuries on previous plays like this one, Fisk took exception to Piniella's actions.

He tagged him with the ball a second time—only harder, and in the jaw.

Lou grabbed the catcher's chest protector to get out from under him, and Fisk rapped him again on the chin, this time with the ball in his right hand. Then the real donnybrook began.

At that moment, Boston first baseman Carl Yastrzemski and Yankee on-deck hitter Sandy Alomar raced to home plate to act as peacemakers.

The rest of the players figured Yastrzemski and Alomar were going to fight, too, so they stormed the diamond with fists cocked.

Bill Lee was the next "outsider" to join the fracas—followed by the Yankees' Velez and Graig Nettles—who put both his arms around the Boston pitcher to try and drag him off the pile-up of players.

"I heard him [Lee] yelling that his shoulder was hurt," Nettles recalled. "If I wanted to punch him right there I could have killed him, but I didn't. At that point, I just wanted to break it up."

Meanwhile, New York outfielder Mickey Rivers, who also had charged out of the dugout to lend physical support, jumped Lee from behind, dragged him to the ground with a hammerlock, and uncorked a number of vicious hammer-like punches in a wind-milling manner.

With Boston's ace left-hander lying on the turf in pain, Nettles tried to explain to a few of Lee's teammates that he only wanted to get him off the pile.

Suddenly Lee got up, walked over to Nettles, and delivered a barrage of invective that made the Yankee third baseman sorry that he even attempted to make peace.

At one point Lee told Nettles, "If you ever hurt my shoulder again, I'll kill you."

That was all the mild-mannered Nettles had to hear.

"He started screaming at me like he was crazy," Graig said. "There were tears in his eyes. He told me he was going to get me, and that's when he started coming after me. I wasn't going to back off any more."

Nettles then connected with a right cross to the eye that decked Lee. They finished their private war on the ground.

By now, the pain in Lee's shoulder was excruciating. Red Sox trainer Charley Moss rushed to the fallen pitcher and escorted him to the dressing room.

It turned out to be Lee's last appearance in uniform for about six weeks.

The rest of the casualty list read like a typical National Football League injury report.

Carl Yastrzemski bruised his foot, and Lou Piniella bruised his hand, but miraculously, the injury-prone Fisk escaped unscathed.

97 | THE SERIES WHERE TWO MANAGERIAL WIVES NEEDED AN APARTMENT

During the 1944 World Series between the St. Louis Browns and St. Louis Cardinals, the wives of respective managers Billy Southworth, of the Cards, and Luke Sewell, of the Brownies, had a problem.

Actually, Sewell and Southworth were on good terms; so good, in fact, that they had an arrangement whereby their respective families shared the same apartment in St. Louis. This was possible during the regular season, since the Browns and Cardinals never were in the city simultaneously. When the Browns (and Luke Sewell) would go on the road, Mrs. Sewell would head for Akron, Ohio, where her family lived.

Each family kept its belongings at different ends of the apartment and the arrangement worked out harmoniously, until both the Cardinals and the Browns won their respective pennants. With both teams camped in St. Louis for the World Series, a problem arose over tenancy of the Lindell Towers apartment, shared by the Southworths and the Sewells.

"It would never do," wrote William B. Mead, author of *Even the Browns*, "for the opposing managers to sit in the same living room after a World Series game, sipping bourbon and chatting politely with their wives. Sewell wanted to invite his mother, and

Mrs. Southworth could hardly be expected to put up with a mother-in-law from the wrong family and, indeed, the wrong League."

The dilemma was resolved when it was learned that another tenant in the building was leaving town for the duration of the World Series. He graciously agreed to allow the Southworths to camp in his abode until the Series was over.

Sewell immediately invited his mother to St. Louis from her home in Alabama. Mrs. Sewell had never seen a big-league ball game in her life, and her proud son was certain that she would be tickled to see him manage in the World Series. Mrs. Sewell arrived in time to see Luke's Browns win the opener, 2–1. She also showed up at Sportsman's Park for Game Two, only this time the Browns lost a heartbreaker, 3–2, in eleven innings.

The Browns' manager recalled with a mixture of bitterness and wry amusement his mother's reaction. "After the second game, I must have stayed up in the clubhouse an hour and a half. Finally, I got out and went to the apartment. My mother likes a rocking chair. Well, I had a rocking chair for her and she was rocking away. I went up, put my arm around her shoulder, and I said, 'Mom, what did you think of that game today?' They had beat us in eleven innings, you know. 'Oh,' she said, 'I was awfully glad when someone won because I was getting mighty tired.'

"It just about broke my heart."

98 | HOW TO LOSE A WORLD SERIES— SIX BLUNDERS ON ONE PLAY, PLUS BAD LUCK ON ANOTHER

When the 1944 World Series between the St. Louis Browns and St. Louis Cardinals was about to begin, sentiment throughout America—if not St. Louis itself—favored the Brownies.

After all, this was their first-ever American League pennant while the Cardinals had done it many times, including in the two previous years and a 1942 World Series win over the New York Yankees.

Better still, the Browns won the opening game, 2–1, and appeared to have the pitching to go all the way.

Ahh, but the fielding. If manager Luke Sewell was missing one important element on the defensive side it was that his fielders were—oh well—better as batters. And nowhere was this more evident than in the Cardinals' half of the third inning of Game Two.

Nelson Potter, one of the season's best pitchers, was dueling Max Lanier of the Cards in what was shaping up as a classic battle of hot hurlers. Now, if only Potter's fielders could just help him out with some rudimentary plays.

Alas, not on this day at Sportsman's Park; not after Emil (The Antelope) Verban singled and Lanier followed with a sacrifice bunt.

What followed was an incredible chain reaction of blunders—six, count 'em, *six*—in rapid succession, that it's a wonder that Sewell didn't follow by pulling every hair out of his head.

How could a team botch up an easy fielding attempt six different times? Here's how:

Lanier's bunt went down the third base line and both Potter and third baseman Mark Christman could have made the easy play. Trouble was that each thought the other would handle the sphere and neither did. Finally Potter took over and, somehow, the ball rubbed up his arm. At this point, the Brownie fielders had gone 0–2, but the best—or worst, in this case—was yet to come.

Potter tossed the ball to first, but second baseman Don Gutteridge, who was covering the bag, covered it too well with his foot, thus being unable to nab the wide throw. Meanwhile, the ball rolled down the right field line, making it 0–3 for the Browns' fielders.

After the ball caromed off the right field wall, right fielder Chet Laabs misplayed the horsehide, which rolled between his legs. 0–4. Manager Sewell, a veteran of many years as both player and manager, thought he had seen everything; but there was more to this fielding horror story. "He (Laabs) picked the ball up," Sewell told author William Mead, "and fumbled it on his pickup, that's five, and threw it away at second base. That's six misplays on one ball."

Eventually, Verban, who had reached third during the blundering, scored and the Cardinals eventually won, 3–2, in a game that by rights—and with a normal fielding team—the Brownies should have annexed.

Or, as other Mead aptly noted, "That play was vintage Brownie stuff."

99 | FIVE STRAIGHT HALL OF FAMERS STRUCK OUT—HOW DID HE DO IT?

When the New York Giants occupied the Polo Grounds in Manhattan's Harlem during the 1930s, the Jints pitching star was a fellow named Carl Hubbell.

A screwball master, Hubbell was so crafty that he owned not one, not two, but three laudable nicknames.

Depending on the day or time of day, Hubbell was known as *King Carl, The Stopper, or The Meal Ticket.*

The monikers were well-earned.

Hubbell set a National League record by pitching forty-six and a third consecutive scoreless innings. He won sixteen games in a row in 1936, and extended that streak to twenty-four when he won the first eight games of the 1937 season. He added a no-run, no-hit game against Pittsburgh and an eighteen-inning game in which he allowed but six hits and no walks. He was the Most Valuable Player, twice, in 1933 and again in '36. Yet his performance in one All-Star Game was so spectacular that it is this single feat most often recalled when the name Carl Hubbell is mentioned.

On July 10, 1934, almost fifty thousand fans watched Hubbell pitch for the National League against an "unbeatable" lineup containing nine future Hall of Famers. Hubbell facing down the likes of Ruth, Gehrig, and Cronin was a lot like David facing several Goliaths!

The American League clearly was a strong favorite. Despite Charley Gehringer's single (he stole second) and Heinie Manush's walk to first, Hubbell remained calm. Babe Ruth came up. Hubbell released his famous screwball and struck him out. The same fate awaited Lou Gehrig, Jimmy Foxx, Al Simmons, and Joe Cronin. Bill Dickey succeeded in hitting a lowly single, upsetting Hubbell's streak.

But the American League won anyway 9–7. Hubbell did not even figure in the decision. Instead, Mel Harder was credited with defeating Van Lingle Mungo.

100 | HOW CAN ANYONE REPLACE THE BABE? WELL, TWINKLETOES DID

In show business, there has been an expression that nobody could follow Madonna's act, or that of Lady Gaga, Frank Sinatra or Don Rickles, for that matter.

Imagine then how difficult it must have been for someone to have followed Babe Ruth's act in the New York Yankees outfield.

Astonishingly, the virtually impossible feat was done—in a matter of speaking—not by an American ballplayer, but one who learned to play the game in Huntsville, Ontario, Canada.

George Selkirk, son of a funeral director, was a very much alive ballplayer whose most notable asset was his speed. Hence, the nickname "Twinkletoes."

Nobody expected Selkirk to wallop the ball in the Ruthian manner, but he won the appreciation of Bombers fans with his fielding and steady—if not overwhelming—hitting. In both 1936 and 1939, Twinkletoes made the American League All-Star Team and batted above the .500 mark on a steady basis.

In the 1936 World Series, Selkirk stepped up to the plate for the first time, facing New York Giants Hall of Fame pitcher Carl Hubbell and promptly swatted a home run.

After retiring as an active player Selkirk became a manager in the minors and later general manager of the Washington Senators in the mid-1960s.

The Canadian ace never was bothered about comparisons with Ruth when fans would introduce him as "The Man Who Replaced the Babe." In fact, Twinkletoes thought it was hilarious one day when a friend introduced the ex-Yankee to his grandson. The lad looked at his grandfather and innocently inquired, "Who's Babe Ruth?"

101 | THE HOBBLED STAR CARRIES A TEAM

When the Dodgers brought in free agent Kirk Gibson after the 1987 season, he brought his leadership ability. He was precisely the veteran the team needed to get over the hump.

Leaving the Tigers was extremely tough for Gibson. "When I left Detroit, a lot was said about me. They attacked me and my character and said things about my family. I remember my parents, especially my dad, defended me. Any father or mother would do that, but I told them, 'Don't worry about it, we'll have our day.'"

In 1988 the Dodgers won the National League West Division with a record of 94–67. They faced a tall order in the National League Championship Series (NLCS), playing against the New York Mets. The Mets were only a few years removed from their improbable 1986 World Series Championship team and had many of the same faces.

The Dodgers struggled against the Mets all season, posting a record of 1–10. Despite the team's failure during the regular season the Dodgers and Gibson were not intimidated.

The Series ended up going seven games. During the series, Gibson smashed two critical home runs and made an incredible catch, falling on the wet turf in left field at Shea Stadium.

They went on to face the dominant Oakland Athletics in the World Series. The A's had a stellar pitching staff, led by Bob Welch, Dennis Eckersley, and Dave Stewart. The A's also had a dynamic offense steered by Mark McGwire and Jose Canseco.

Two of the most feared attributes in baseball are pitching and power. The Oakland team had an abundance of both of them.

Oakland A's outfielder Don Baylor gave the Dodgers plenty of motivation by saying, "The Mets were the better team, and I wanted to play the better team. I was with the Boston Red Sox in 1986, and I wanted another shot at them after they beat us. I wanted another shot at the Mets."

After getting injured in the NLCS, the common belief was Gibson would not be able to play.

As announcer Bob Costas said, "I remember coming on the air and saying, 'First item of business: Kirk Gibson will not play tonight.' We had been told he was out. That was how we set the stage for Game One."

In Game One, the Dodgers were behind by one run heading into the ninth inning. With two outs and the base-path empty, Mike Davis was due up at the plate. Davis had plenty of power to tie the game; Eckersley decided to pitch around Davis. Dave Anderson was in the on-deck circle; he was not known for his offense.

After the Davis walk, Tommy Lasorda, the Dodgers manager, called Anderson back to the bench, and a hobbled Gibson emerged from the Dodger dugout. He had spent the entire game in the clubhouse getting treatment on his leg.

Vin Scully, the legendary Dodger broadcaster, had told the TV audience "that Gibson wasn't in the dugout and for sure wouldn't be playing."

Gibson hobbled to the plate to an incredible ovation. "The crowd," Lasorda said. "I can never explain it. The emotion, the reaction of that crowd on that night. I've been here a long time; I've never seen anything like that. I got goose bumps because of the reaction of the fans."

As Gibson limped to the plate he told himself, "The ovation and the environment would be outstanding and I wouldn't hurt anymore, and it was true."

"He fouled away the first two pitches, and, after he swung, he looked so feeble," Eckersley said. "I thought I was going to blow him away. I thought he was a lamb, I'm thinking I'm going to throw him a high fastball and he's done."

Gibson battled at the plate, working the count back to 2–2. Davis was able to steal second base, putting the game-tying run in scoring position.

Gibson extended his arms and belted a backdoor slider over the right field fence. It was one of the greatest home runs in World Series history. Gibson limped around the bases, and the crowd was ecstatic.

The Dodgers went on to win the series in five games after the improbable Gibson home run. Gibson's gimpy home run trot around the bases remains one of the most iconic moments in Major League Baseball history.

EPILOGUE

You win some; you lose some.

My baseball-rooting for the year 2013 extended into the playoffs, during which time I first focused my attention on my favorite club, the Oakland Athletics. And for a short time, I believed that they just might defeat the Detroit Tigers. As it happens, one of my closest pals in baseball—and hockey—happens to be Jimmy Devellano, who is executive vice president of the Tigers, as well as veep of the Detroit Red Wings.

Naturally, I phoned Jimmy D before the series and explained that I couldn't, in good conscience, wish his club well to the detriment of my A's. He understood, and his Tigers went on to eliminate Oakland, fair and square, I might add. The defeat did not bother me very much, nor for very long because: 1. The Athletics invariably do better than most folks believe that they will; and 2. They have the best-looking uniforms in baseball, which means that Oakland fans always have something to be happy about, win or lose.

I then moved my cheering attention over to the St. Louis Cardinals—always thinking of my heroes, Stan (The Man) Musial, Enos (Country) Slaughter, and Johnny (Hippety) Hopp. For a time, it appeared that the Cards would defeat the annoying Red

Sox, but that delightful event was not to be and, thus, my 2013 baseball season ended again, on a pleasant note, since the Cards have given me plenty of thrills in this decade alone.

But baseball never really leaves my head. When the season ends, it's time for the Hot Stove League, and nothing is more pleasant than opening a book about the diamond sport between October and spring training. With that in mind, I'm presenting for your reading—and learning—pleasure, my baseball bibliography. Most of the following books helped me, in one form or another, to produce the collection of baseball stories that fit between these covers. I heartily recommend any or all of them for your enjoyment.

I must—in all fairness—point out that my personal three favorites are: 1. *Even the Browns*, by Bill Mead; 2. *Baseball When the Grass Was Green*, by Donald Honig; and 3. *Baseball Between the Lines*, also by Honig.

BIBLIOGRAPHY

Allen, Lee. *The Hot Stove League*. New York, NY: A. S. Barnes and Company, 1955.

Astor, Gerald, and Roy Blount. *The Baseball Hall of Fame 50th Anniversary Book*. New York, NY: Prentice Hall, 1988.

Barthel, Thomas. *Baseball's Peerless Semipros: The Brooklyn Bushwicks of Dexter Park*. Haworth, NJ: St. Johann, 2009.

Borst, Bill, Jim Scott, and George Walden. *Ables to Zoldak St. Louis Browns Vol. II*. St. Louis, MO: St. Louis Browns Press, 1989.

Chen, Albert. "The Greatest Game Ever Pitched." *Fifty Years Ago Harvey Haddix Threw 12 Perfect*. N.p., 1 June 2009. Web.

Davis, Mac. *Sports Shorts, Astonishing, Strange but True*. New York, NY: Bantam, 1959.

Dewey, Donald, and Nick Acocella. *Encyclopedia of Major League Baseball Teams*. New York, NY: HarperCollins, 1993.

Einstein, Charles. *The Baseball Reader*. New York, NY: McGraw-Hill Book Company, 1955.

Fehler, Gene. *Tales from Baseball's Golden Age*. Champaign, IL: Sports Pub., 2000.

Fischler, Stan. *Showdown: Baseball's Ultimate Confrontations*. New York, NY: Grosset and Dunlap, 1978.

Fischler, Stan, and Shirley Fischler. *The Best, Worst and Most Unusual in Sports*. New York, NY: Crowell, 1977.

Fischler, Stan, and Shirley Fischler. *Stan Fischler's Amazing Trivia from the World of Baseball*. Markham, Ont.: Penguin, 1984.

Fischler, Stan, and Richard Friedman. *The Comeback Yankees*. New York, NY: Grosset and Dunlap, 1979.

Goldstein, Richard. *Spartan Seasons: How Baseball Survived the Second World War*. New York, NY: Macmillan, 1980.

Graham, Frank. *Casey Stengel: His Half-Century in Baseball*. New York, NY: John Day, 1958.

Gutman, Dan. *Baseball's Biggest Bloopers: The Games That Got Away*. New York, NY: Viking, 1993.

Honig, Donald. *Baseball between the Lines: Baseball in the '40s and '50s as Told by the Men Who Played It*. New York, NY: Coward, McCann & Geoghegan, 1976.

Honig, Donald. *Baseball When the Grass Was Real: Baseball from the Twenties to the Forties Told by the Men Who Played It*. New York, NY: Coward, McCann & Geoghegan, 1975.

Honig, Donald. *The October Heroes: Great World Series Games Remembered by the Men Who Played Them*. New York, NY: Simon and Schuster, 1979.

Honig, Donald. *The World Series: An Illustrated History from 1903 to the Present*. New York, NY: Crown, 1986.

Kaplan, Jim. "Nearly Half Century Later, Spahn-Marichal Duel Still the Best Ever."*Warren Spahn-Juan Marichal 1963 Duel Still Best Ever*. N.p., 1 July 2011. Web.

Kurkjian, Tim. "Remembering the Amazing Ted Williams." *ESPN*. ESPN Internet Ventures, 28 Sept. 2011. Web.

Lowry, Philip J. *Green Cathedrals: The Ultimate Celebration of All 271 Major League and Negro League Ballparks Past and Present*. Reading, MA: Addison-Wesley Pub., 1992.

Mazer, Bill, and Stan Fischler. *The Amazin' Bill Mazer's Baseball Trivia Book*. New York, NY: Warner, 1981.

Mead, William B., *Baseball Goes to War*. Washington, D.C.: Contemporary Books, Inc., 1978

Meany, Tom. *The Artful Dodgers*. New York, NY: A.S. Barnes, 1953.

Meany, Tom. *Baseball's Greatest Teams,*. New York, NY: A.S. Barnes, 1949.

Morgan, Dan. *The Complete Baseball Joke Book*. New York, NY: Stravon Publishers., 1953.

Okrent, Daniel, and Steve Wulf. *Baseball Anecdotes*. New York, NY: Oxford UP, 1989.

Peterson, John E. *The Kansas City Athletics: A Baseball History, 1954–1967*. Jefferson, NC: McFarland, 2003.

Pope, Edwin. *Baseball's Greatest Managers*. Garden City, NY: Doubleday, 1960.

Prince, Carl E. *Brooklyn's Dodgers: The Bums, the Borough, and the Best of Baseball, 1947–1957*. New York, NY: Oxford UP, 1996.

Reichler, Joseph L., and Ben Olan. *Baseball's Unforgettable Games*. New York, NY: Ronald, 1960.

Rose, Howie, and Phil Pepe. *Put It In the Book!: A Half-Century of Mets Mania*. Chicago, IL: Triumph Books, 2013.

Schiffer, Don. *World Series Encyclopedia*. New York, NY: Nelson, 1961.

Sugar, Bert Randolph. *Baseball's 50 Greatest Games*. New York, NY: Exeter, 1986.